Numsense! Data Science for the Layman

No Math Added

Annalyn Ng and Kenneth Soo

Numsense! Data Science for the Layman

No Math Added

Annalyn Ng and Kenneth Soo

ISBN 978-981-11-1068-9

First edition, 2017

Contents

Foreword

Big data is now big business. With our lives increasingly dominated by data, monetizing these data has become a focal point of nearly every organization. Techniques to recognize patterns and make predictions are providing new dimensions of business capabilities. Product recommendation systems, for instance, are a win-win for both sellers and customers as they alert customers to products they are likely to be interested in, which in turn rakes in higher profits for sellers.

But big data is only one piece of the puzzle. Data science, which allows us to analyze and leverage data, is a multifaceted discipline which encompasses machine learning, statistics and related branches of mathematics. Note that machine learning holds a particularly elevated position in this description, being the primary engine that enables pattern recognition and predictive capabilities. When paired with data, the machine learning algorithms which power data science can lead to invaluable insights and new ways of harnessing the information already at our fingertips.

To appreciate how data science is driving the present data revolution, there is a need for the uninitiated to gain a better understanding of this field. However, apprehensiveness over prerequisite skills have caused some to shun the field despite the high demand for data literacy.

This is where *Numsense: Data Science for the Layman* comes in. Having been familiar with the work of Annalyn Ng and Kenneth Soo for some time, it comes as no surprise that the book delivers on its titular promise. This *is* data science for the layman, and the often-complex math—which the book describes at a high level—is intentionally not covered in detail. But don't be misled: this does not mean that the contents are in any way watered down. In fact, the information contained within is robust, with its strength being that it is abridged and concise.

What good does this approach do, you may ask? Well, quite a lot, actually! I would argue that, for the layman, this approach is preferable. Think of a layman interested in learning about automobile operation: a high-level overview of automobile components would likely be less overwhelming than a technical text on combustion physics. The same goes for introductory data science: if you are interested in learning about the field, it is easier to start with broad concepts before drilling down into mathematical formulas.

The book's introduction gets the uninitiated up to speed on fundamental concepts in a few pages, ensuring that everyone begins the book with a common foundation of what data science is. Important concepts such as algorithm selection—often overlooked in introductory materials—are also covered straight away, instilling in readers a sense of urgency to complete their understanding of the field, while supplying a comprehensive framework to do so.

There are all sorts of concepts that Annalyn and Kenneth could have deemed worthy of treatment in their book, and a number of ways in which they could have addressed presentation. Their approach of focusing mainly on the machine learning algorithms of greatest importance to data science, with a few task-based scenarios thrown in, was a great decision. Tried and tested algorithms like k-means clustering, decision trees, and nearest neighbors are given their due. More recent state-of-the-art classification and ensemble algorithms such as support vector machines—often intimidating due to their complex mathematics—and random forests are explained as well. Neural networks, the driving force behind the current deep learning frenzy, are also covered.

Pairing algorithms with intuitive use cases is another strength of *Numsense*. Be it explaining random forests in the context of forecasting crime, or clustering as it relates to profiling movie fans, the examples chosen provide clarity and practical understanding. At the same time, sparing any mention of high level math sustains the interest and motivation of what is assumed to be a reader's initial foray into the study of data science.

I highly recommend *Numsense: Data Science for the Layman* to beginners looking for an entry point into data science or the algorithms that drive it. I would find it difficult to name a comparable material. With *Numsense*, there is no reason to let the math keep you away any longer.

Matthew Mayo
Data Scientist and Deputy Editor of KDnuggets
@mattmayo13

Preface

Numsense is dedicated to you by two data science enthusiasts, Annalyn Ng (University of Cambridge) and Kenneth Soo (Stanford University).

We noticed that while data science is increasingly used to improve workplace decisions, many know little about the field. Hence, we compiled these tutorials into a book so that more people can learn—be it an aspiring student, enterprising business professional, or anyone with a curious mind.

Each tutorial covers the important functions and assumptions of a data science technique, free from math and jargon. We also illustrate these techniques with real-world data and examples.

We could not have written this book on our own.

We thank Sonya Chan, our copyeditor and a good friend, for skillfully melding our writing styles and ensuring that our narrative flows seamlessly.

We thank Dora Tan for advice on the book's layout and graphics.

We thank our friends Michelle Poh, Dennis Chew and Mark Ho for invaluable suggestions on how to improve the comprehensibility of our content.

We also thank Prof. Long Nguyen (University of Michigan, Ann Arbor), Prof. Percy Liang (Stanford University) and Dr. Michal Kosinski (Stanford University) for their patience in nurturing us and for sharing their expert advice.

Finally, both of us would like to thank each other, for bickering like good friends do, but always sticking around till the end to finish what we started.

Why Data Science?

Imagine yourself as a young doctor.

A patient enters your clinic, complaining of breathlessness, chest pains, and the occasional heartburn. You check that his blood pressure and heart rate readings are normal, and that he has had no previous medical conditions.

Sizing him up, you notice that he looks plump. As his symptoms are common among people who are overweight, you reassure him that everything is under control and recommend that he finds time to exercise.

All too often, this situation results in a misdiagnosis of heart disease—as patients with heart disease exhibit symptoms similar to those of common obesity, doctors often pass over further checks that would detect the more serious condition.

As humans, our judgements are constrained by limited, subjective experiences and incomplete knowledge. This impairs our decision-making process and could, as in the case of an inexperienced doctor, arrest further tests that would have led to more accurate conclusions.

This is where data science can help.

Instead of relying on the judgement of one individual, data science techniques allow us to harness information from more data sources to make better decisions. For instance, we could check historical records of patients reporting similar symptoms to uncover possible diagnoses that were previously overlooked.

With modern computing and advanced algorithms, we are able to:

- Identify hidden trends in large datasets
- Leverage trends to make predictions
- Compute the probability of each possible outcome
- Obtain accurate results quickly

This book has been written in layman's terms (no math here!) as a gentle introduction to data science and its algorithms. To help you grasp key concepts, we stick to intuitive explanations and lots of visuals.

Each algorithm has its own dedicated chapter, featuring a real-world example application that explains how the algorithm works. Data used for these examples are available online, and their sources are listed in the references section.

If you need to revisit what you had learned, check out the summaries after each chapter. At the end of the book, you will also find handy reference sheets comparing the pros and cons of each algorithm, as well as a glossary list of commonly-used terms.

With this book, we hope to give you a practical understanding of data science, so that you, too, can leverage its strengths to make better decisions.

Let's get started.

1. Basics in a Nutshell

To fully appreciate how data science algorithms work, we must start from the basics. This introduction is thus the longest chapter in this book, running over twice as long as subsequent chapters that dwell on actual algorithms. However, through this introduction, you will gain a solid overview of the fundamental steps involved in almost all data science research. These basic processes will help you assess the context, as well as constraints, for selecting suitable algorithms to use in a study.

There are four key steps in a data science study. First, the data must be processed and prepared for analysis. Next, suitable algorithms are shortlisted based on our study's requirements. Following which, parameters of the algorithms have to be tuned to optimize results. These finally culminate in the building of models that are then compared to select the best one.

1.1 Data Preparation

Data science is all about the data. If data quality is poor, even the most sophisticated analysis would generate only lackluster results. In this section, we will cover the basic data format typically used in analysis, as well as methods for data processing to improve results.

Data Format

The tabular form is most commonly used to represent data for analysis (see Table 1). Each row indicates a *data point* representing a single observation, and each column shows a *variable* describing the data point. Variables are also known as *attributes*, *features*, or *dimensions*.

Variables

Data Points

Transaction ID	Customer Species	Date	Fruits Bought	Fish Bought	Amount Spent
1	Penguin	Jan 1st	1	Yes	\$5.30
2	Bear	Jan 1st	4	Yes	\$9.70
3	Rabbit	Jan 1st	6	No	\$6.50
4	Horse	Jan 2nd	6	No	\$5.50
5	Penguin	Jan 2nd	2	Yes	\$6.00
6	Giraffe	Jan 3rd	5	No	\$4.80
7	Rabbit	Jan 3rd	8	No	\$7.60
8	Cat	Jan 3rd	?	Yes	\$7.40

Table 1. Imaginary dataset of grocery transactions from animals shopping at a supermarket. Each row is a transaction, and each column provides information on the transactions.

Depending on our objective, we could change the type of observations represented in each row. For instance, the representation in Table 1 allows us to study patterns across a number of transactions. However, if we instead wanted to study transaction patterns across days, we need to represent each row as an aggregate of the day's transactions. For a more comprehensive analysis, we could also add new variables, such as the day's weather (see Table 2).

Variables

Date	Amount Earned	No. of Customers	Weather	Weekend
Jan 1st	\$21.50	3	Sunny	Yes
Jan 2nd	\$11.50	2	Rainy	No
Jan 3rd	\$19.80	3	Sunny	No

Table 2. Reformatted dataset showing aggregated daily transactions, with additional variables included.

Variable Types

There are four main types of variables, and it is important to distinguish between them to ensure that they are appropriate for our selected algorithms.

- **Binary**. This is the simplest type of variable, with only two possible options. In Table 1, a binary variable is used to indicate if customers bought fish.
- **Categorical**. When there are more than two options, the information can be represented via a categorical variable. In Table 1, a categorical variable is used to describe the customers' species.
- **Integer**. These are used when the information can be represented as a whole number. In Table 1, an integer variable is used to indicate the number of fruits purchased by each customer.
- **Continuous**. This is the most detailed variable, representing numbers with decimal places. In Table 1, a continuous variable is used to indicate the amount spent by each customer.

Variable Selection

While we might be handed an original dataset that contains many variables, throwing too many variables into an algorithm might lead to slow computation, or wrong predictions due to excess noise. Hence, we need to shortlist the important variables.

Selecting variables is often a trial-and-error process, with variables swapped in or out based on feedback from our results. As a start, we can use simple plots to examine correlations (see Chapter 6.5) between variables, with promising ones selected for further analysis.

Feature Engineering

Sometimes, however, the best variables need to be engineered. For example, if we wanted to predict which customers in Table 1 would avoid fish, we could look at the customer species variable to determine that rabbits, horses and giraffes would not purchase fish. Nonetheless, if we had grouped customer species into broader categories of herbivores, omnivores and carnivores, we could reach a more generalized conclusion: herbivores do not buy fish.

Besides recoding a single variable, we could also combine multiple variables in a technique known as dimension reduction, which will be covered in Chapter 3. Dimension reduction can be used to extract the most useful information and condense that into a new but smaller set of variables for analysis.

Missing Data

It is not always possible to collect complete data. In Table 1, for example, the number of fruits purchased in the last transaction was not recorded. Missing data can interfere with analysis, and so should be—whenever possible—handled in one of the following ways:

- **Approximated**. If the missing value is of either the binary or categorical variable type, it could be replaced with the mode (i.e. the most common value) of that variable. For integers or continuous values, the median could be used. Applying this method to Table 1 would allow us to estimate that the cat bought five fruits, as that was the median number of fruits purchased in the other seven transactions.

- **Computed**. Missing values could also be computed using more advanced algorithms under supervised learning (to be covered in the next section). While more time-consuming, computed estimates tend to be more accurate because the algorithms estimate missing values based on similar transactions, unlike the approximation method that reviews every transaction. From Table 1, we can observe that customers who bought fish tended to purchase fewer fruits, and hence estimate that the cat only bought about two or three fruits.

- **Removed**. As a last resort, rows with missing values could be removed. However, this is generally avoided as it reduces the amount of data available for analysis. Moreover, excluding data points could cause the resulting data sample to be skewed toward or away from particular groups. For instance, cats might be less willing to disclose the number of fruits they purchase, and if we removed customers with unrecorded fruit transactions, cats would then be under-represented in our final sample.

After the dataset has been processed, it would be time for us to analyze it.

1.2 Algorithm Selection

In this book, we will discuss over ten different algorithms that can be used to analyze data. The choice of algorithm depends on the type of task we wish to perform, of which there are three main categories. Table 3 lists the algorithms which will be covered in this book, as well as their associated categories.

	Algorithms
Unsupervised Learning	*k*-Means Clustering Principal Component Analysis Association Rules Social Network Analysis
Supervised Learning	Regression Analysis *k*-Nearest Neighbors Support Vector Machine Decision Tree Random Forests Neural Networks
Reinforcement Learning	Multi-Armed Bandits

Table 3. Algorithms and their corresponding categories.

Unsupervised Learning

Task: *Tell me what patterns exist in my data.*

When we want to find hidden patterns in our dataset, we could use *unsupervised learning* algorithms. These algorithms are unsupervised because we do not know what patterns to look out for and thus leave them to be uncovered by the algorithm.

In Table 1, an unsupervised model could learn which items were frequently bought together (using association rules, explained in Chapter 4), or it could cluster customers based on their purchases (explained in Chapter 2).

We could validate results from an unsupervised model via indirect means, such as checking if customer clusters generated correspond to familiar categories (e.g. herbivores and carnivores).

Supervised Learning

Task: *Use the patterns in my data to make predictions.*

When we want to make predictions, *supervised learning* algorithms could be used. These algorithms are supervised because we want them to base their predictions on pre-existing patterns.

In Table 1, a supervised model could learn to forecast the number of fruits a customer would purchase (*prediction*) based on its species and whether it bought fish (*predictor variables*).

We can directly assess the accuracy of a supervised model by inputting values for species and fish purchase for future customers, and then checking how close the model's predictions are to the actual numbers of fruits bought.

When we predict integers or continuous values, such as the number of fruits purchased, we would be solving a *regression* problem (see Figure 1a). When we predict binary or categorical values, such as whether it would rain or not, we would be solving a *classification* problem (see Figure 1b). Nonetheless, most classification algorithms are also able to generate predictions as a continuous probability value, such as in statements like "*there is a 75% chance of rain*", which allows for predictions of higher precision.

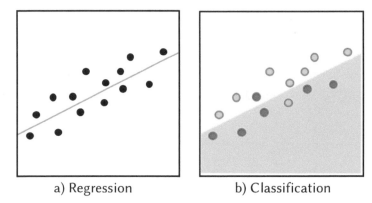

a) Regression   b) Classification

Figure 1. Regression involves deriving a trend line, while classification involves categorizing data points into groups. Note that errors would be expected in both tasks. In regression, data points might stray from the trend line, while in classification, data points might fall into wrong categories.

Reinforcement Learning

Task: *Use the patterns in my data to make predictions, and improve these predictions as more results come in.*

Unlike unsupervised and supervised learning, where models are learned and then deployed without further changes, a *reinforcement learning* model continuously improves itself using feedback from results.

Moving away from Table 1 to a real-life example: imagine we are comparing the effectiveness of two online ads. We could initially display each ad equally often, assessing the number of people who clicked on each ad. A reinforcement learning model would then take this number as feedback on the ad's popularity, using it to tweak the display to favor the more popular ad. Through this iterative process, the model could eventually learn to display the better ad exclusively.

Other Considerations

Besides the main tasks they perform, algorithms also differ in other aspects, such as their ability to analyze different data types, as well as the nature of results they generate. These are covered in the subsequent chapters dedicated to each algorithm, and also listed in summary tables found in Appendix A (for unsupervised learning) and Appendix B (for supervised learning).

1.3 Parameter Tuning

The numerous algorithms available in data science naturally translate to a vast number of potential models we could build—but even a single algorithm can generate varying results, depending on how its parameters are tuned.

Parameters are options used to tweak an algorithm's settings, much like tuning a radio for the right frequency channel. Different algorithms have different parameters available for tuning. For common tuning parameters associated with algorithms covered in this book, see Appendix C.

Needless to say, a model's accuracy suffers when its parameters are not suitably tuned. Take a look at Figure 2 to observe how one classification algorithm could generate multiple boundaries to distinguish between orange and blue points.

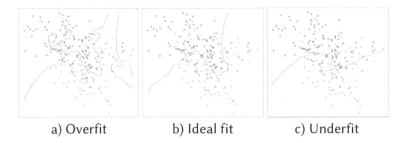

a) Overfit   b) Ideal fit   c) Underfit

Figure 2. Comparison of prediction results from the same algorithm fitted with different parameters.

In Figure 2a, the algorithm was overly-sensitive and mistook random variations in the data as persistent patterns. This problem is known as *overfitting*. An overfitted model would yield highly accurate predictions for the current data, but would be less generalizable to future data.

In Figure 2c, on the other hand, the algorithm was too insensitive, and overlooked underlying patterns. This problem is known as *underfitting*. An underfitted model is likely to neglect significant trends, which would cause it to yield less accurate predictions for both current and future data.

But when parameters are tuned just right, such as shown in Figure 2b, the algorithm strikes a balance between identifying major trends and discounting minor variations, rendering the resulting model well-suited for making predictions.

For most studies, overfitting is a constant concern. In seeking to minimize prediction errors, we may be tempted to increase the complexity of our prediction model, which eventually leads to results like those in Figure 2a—prediction boundaries that are intricate but superfluous.

One way to keep a model's overall complexity in check is to introduce a penalty parameter, in a step known as *regularization*. This new parameter penalizes any increase in a model's complexity by artificially inflating prediction error, thus enabling the algorithm to account for both complexity and accuracy in optimizing its original parameters. By keeping a model simple, we help to maintain its generalizability.

1.4 Evaluating Results

After building a model, it must be evaluated. Evaluation metrics are used to compare how accurate models are in their predictions. These metrics differ in how they define and penalize different types of prediction errors.

Below are three evaluation metrics that are used frequently. Depending on the aims of our study, new metrics could even be designed to penalize and avoid specific types of errors. As such, the list of evaluation metrics covered in this book is by no means exhaustive. For more examples of metrics, see Appendix D.

Classification Metrics

Percentage of Correct Predictions. The most simplistic definition of prediction accuracy is the proportion of predictions that proved to be correct. Going back to our example on grocery transactions in Table 1, we could express results from an example task to predict fish purchase in a statement like: *Our model predicting whether a customer would buy fish was correct 90% of the time.* While this metric is easy to understand, it leaves out information about where prediction errors actually occur.

Confusion Matrix. Confusion matrices provide further insight into where our prediction model succeeded and where it failed.

		Prediction	
		Will buy	Will not buy
Actual	Bought	1 (TP)	5 (FN)
	Did not buy	5 (FP)	89 (TN)

Table 4. Confusion matrix showing accuracy of an example task to predict fish purchase.

Take a look at Table 4. While the model had an overall classification accuracy of 90%, it was much better at predicting non-purchases than actual purchases. We can also see that prediction errors were split equally between *false positives (FP)* and *false negatives (FN)*, with five errors each.

In some situations, distinguishing the type of prediction error is crucial. A false negative in earthquake prediction (i.e. predicting no earthquake would happen but it does) would be far costlier than false positives (i.e. predicting an earthquake would happen but it does not).

Regression Metric

Root Mean Squared Error (RMSE). As regression predictions use continuous values, errors are generally quantified as the difference between predicted and actual values, with penalties varying with the magnitude of error. The *root mean squared error* (RMSE) is a popular regression metric, and is particularly useful in cases where we want to avoid large errors: each individual error is squared, thus amplifying large errors. This renders the RMSE extremely sensitive to outliers, of which are severely penalized.

Validation

Metrics do not give a complete picture of a model's performance. Due to overfitting (see Chapter 1.3), models which fare well on a metric for current data might not do so for new data. To prevent this, we should always evaluate models using a proper validation procedure.

Validation is an assessment of how accurate a model is in predicting new data. However, instead of waiting for new data to assess our model, we could split our current dataset into two parts: the first part would serve as a *training dataset* to generate and tune a prediction model, while the second part would act as a proxy for new data and be used as a *test dataset* to assess the model's prediction accuracy. The best model is taken to be the one yielding the most accurate predictions on the test dataset. For this validation process to be effective, we should assign data points into the training and test datasets randomly and without bias.

However, if the original dataset is small, we may not have the luxury of setting aside data to form a test dataset, because we may sacrifice accuracy when the amount of data used to train our model is reduced. Hence, instead of using two separate datasets for training and testing, cross-validation would allow us to use one dataset for both purposes.

Cross-validation maximizes the availability of data for validation by dividing the dataset into several segments that are used to test the model repeatedly. In a single iteration, all but one of the segments would be used to train a predictive model, which is then tested on the last segment. This process is repeated until each segment has been used as the test segment exactly once (see Figure 3).

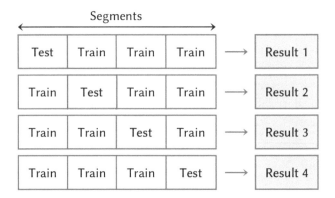

Figure 3. Cross-validation of a dataset. The dataset has been divided into four segments, and the final prediction accuracy is the average of the four results.

As different segments are used to generate predictions for each iteration, the resulting predictions would vary. By accounting for such variations, we can achieve a more robust estimate of a model's actual predictive ability. The final estimate of a model's accuracy is taken as the average of that across all iterations.

If results from cross-validation suggest that our model's prediction accuracy is low, we can go back to re-tune the parameters or re-processed the data.

1.5 Summary

There are four key steps in a data science study:

1. Prepare data
2. Select algorithms to model the data
3. Tune algorithms to optimize the models
4. Evaluate models based on their accuracy

2. k-Means Clustering

2.1 Finding Customer Clusters

Let's talk about movie preferences. Take for instance a person who likes *50 First Dates*—it is highly likely that he or she would also enjoy similar chick flicks such as *27 Dresses*. This is how clustering works: by identifying common preferences or characteristics, it is possible to sort customers into groups, which retailers may then use for targeted advertisement.

However, identifying customer groups is tricky. We may not know initially how customers should be grouped, nor how many groups exist.

A technique known as *k-means clustering* could answer these questions. This method can be used to group customers or products in distinct clusters, where k represents the number of clusters identified.

2.2 Example: Personality Profiles of Movie Fans

To identify customer clusters via k-means clustering, we need quantifiable customer information. A common variable is income, since higher-income groups tend to purchase more branded products as compared to lower-income groups. As such, stores can use this information to direct advertisements of expensive products toward higher-income groups.

Personality traits are also a good way to group customers—as done in the following survey of Facebook users. Users were invited to complete a questionnaire in order to check how they scored on four personality traits: *extraversion* (how much they enjoyed social interactions), *conscientiousness* (how hardworking they were), *emotionality* (how often they got stressed) and *openness* (how receptive they were to novelty).

Initial analysis revealed positive associations among these personality traits. Highly conscientious people were likely to be more extraverted, and, to a smaller extent, highly emotional people tended to be more open. Hence, to better visualize these personality traits, we paired them—conscientiousness with extraversion, and emotionality with openness—and aggregated scores within each pair, before marking them on a 2-dimensional plot.

The aggregated personality scores for each person were then matched against the movie pages he or she had 'liked' on Facebook, hence allowing us to identify groups of movie fans by their distinct personality profiles (see Figure 1).

In Figure 1, we observe two main clusters:

- **Red**: Conscientious extraverts who like action and romance genres
- **Blue**: Emotional and open people who like avant-garde and fantasy genres

And beyond those clusters, movies in the center appear to be general household favorites.

With such information, targeted advertisements can be designed. If a person likes *50 First Dates*, a storekeeper can easily recommend another movie in the same cluster, or even bundle similar products for effective discounts.

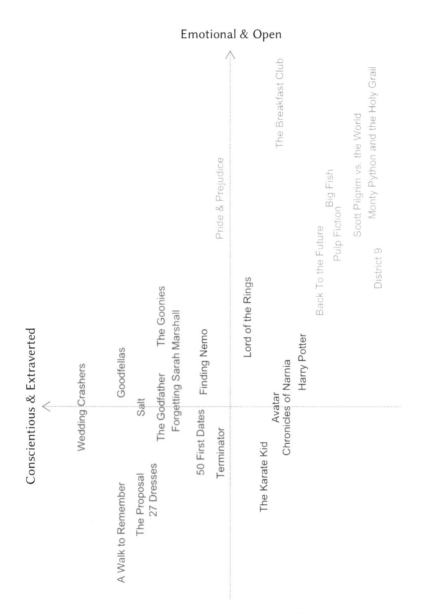

Figure 1. Personality profiles of movie fans.

2.3 Defining Clusters

In defining clusters, we have to answer two questions: How many clusters exist? And what is the membership of each cluster?

How many clusters exist?

This is subjective. While Figure 1 shows two clusters, these could be further broken down into smaller clusters. For instance, the blue cluster could have sub-clusters of a drama genre (comprising *Pride & Prejudice* and *The Breakfast Club*) as well as a fantasy genre (comprising *Monty Python and the Holy Grail* and *Scott Pilgrim vs. the World*).

As the number of clusters increases, members within each cluster become more similar to each other, but neighboring clusters also become less distinct from each other. Taking this to the extreme, each data point could become a cluster in itself, which provides us with no useful information at all.

So obviously, a balance must be struck. The number of clusters should be large enough to enable us to extract meaningful patterns that can inform business decisions, but also small enough to ensure that clusters remain clearly distinct.

One way to determine the appropriate number of clusters is to use a scree plot (see Figure 2).

A *scree plot* shows how within-cluster scatter decreases as the number of clusters increases. If all members belong to a single cluster, within-cluster scatter would be at its maximum. As we increase the number of clusters, clusters grow more compact and their members more homogenous.

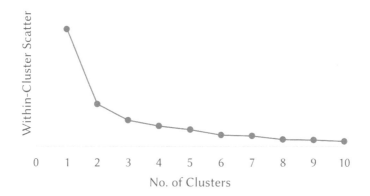

Figure 2. Scree plot showing 'kinks' indicating the presence of two to three clusters.

A *kink* is a sharp bend in the scree plot that suggests an optimal number of clusters to derive, such that within-cluster scatter is reduced to a reasonable degree. In Figure 2, we see a kink where the number of clusters equals to two, corresponding to the two main movie clusters in Figure 1. Another shallower kink is located where the number of clusters equals to three, suggesting that we could also include a third cluster of household favorites. Beyond this, generating more clusters would yield smaller clusters that are more difficult to distinguish from each other.

After establishing a suitable number of clusters, we can then determine the membership of each.

What is the membership of each cluster?

Cluster membership is determined in an iterative process, which is summarized with the 2-cluster example illustrated in Figure 3.

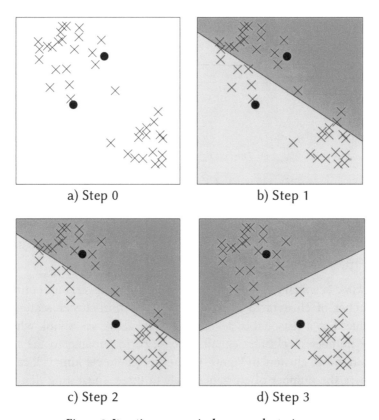

a) Step 0   b) Step 1

c) Step 2   d) Step 3

Figure 3. Iterative process in *k*-means clustering.

Since a good cluster would comprise closely packed data points, we could assess the validity of a cluster by verifying how far its members are from the cluster's center. However, since the positions of cluster centers are unknown initially, they are first approximated. Data points would then be assigned to their closest cluster centers.

Following this, cluster centers would be re-positioned to the actual centers of their members, before cluster membership of each data point is once again assigned based on distance—if a data point happens to be far from its assigned cluster's center and closer to that of a neighboring cluster, its membership would be re-assigned.

The following steps neatly summarize the process of determining cluster membership, and can be used for any number of clusters.

Step 0: Start by guessing where the central points of each cluster are. Let's call these pseudo-centers, since we do not yet know if they are actually at the center of their clusters.

Step 1: Assign each data point to the nearest pseudo-center. By doing so, we have formed two clusters, red and blue.

Step 2: Update the location of the pseudo-centers to the center of their respective members.

Step 3: Repeat the steps of cluster member re-assignments (Step 1) and cluster center re-positioning (Step 2), until there are no more changes to cluster membership.

Although we have only covered 2-dimensional analysis, clustering can also be done in three or more dimensions. These additional dimensions could, for a storekeeper, constitute a customer's age or frequency of visit. While difficult to visualize, we can rely on computing programs to calculate multi-dimensional distances between data points and cluster centers.

2.4 Limitations

Although k-means clustering can be useful, it is not without limitation:

Each data point can only be assigned to one cluster. Sometimes a data point might be in the middle of two clusters, with an equal probability of being assigned to either.

Clusters are assumed to be spherical. The iterative process of finding data points closest to a cluster center is akin to narrowing the cluster's radius, so that the resulting cluster resembles a compact sphere. This might pose a problem if the shape of an actual cluster is, for instance, an ellipse—such elongated clusters might be truncated, with their members subsumed into nearby clusters.

Clusters are assumed to be discrete. *k*-means clustering does not permit clusters to overlap, nor to be nested within each other.

Instead of coercing each data point into a single cluster, there are more robust clustering techniques that compute the probabilities of how likely each data point might belong to other clusters, thus helping to identify non-spherical or overlapping clusters.

However, despite these constraints, the strength of the *k*-means clustering algorithm lies in its elegant simplicity. A good strategy might be to start with *k*-means clustering for a basic understanding of the data structure, before delving into more advanced methods to mitigate its limitations.

2.5 Summary

- *k*-means clustering is a technique to group similar data points together. The number of clusters, *k*, must be specified in advance.
- To cluster data points, first assign each point to the nearest cluster, and then update the position of cluster centers. Repeat these two steps until there are no further changes in cluster membership.
- *k*-means clustering works best for spherical, non-overlapping clusters.

3. Principal Component Analysis

3.1 Exploring Nutritional Content of Food

Imagine that you are a nutritionist. What is the best way to differentiate between food items? By vitamin content? Protein levels? Or perhaps a combination of both?

Figure 1. Simple food pyramid.

Knowing the variables that best differentiate your items has several uses:

- **Visualization**. Plotting items with the right variables could help you gain more insight.
- **Uncovering Clusters**. With good visualization, hidden categories or clusters could be uncovered. In food items, for instance, we could identify broad categories such as meat and

vegetables, in addition to sub-categories for different types of vegetables.

The question is, how do we derive the variables that best differentiate between our items?

3.2 Principal Components

Principal Component Analysis (PCA) is a technique that finds the underlying variables (known as *principal components*) that best differentiate your data points. These principal components are dimensions along which your data points are most spread out (see Figure 2).

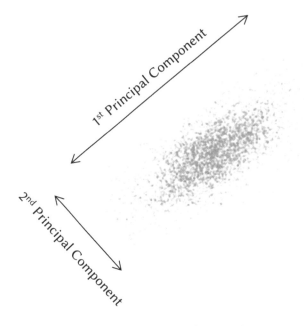

Figure 2. Visual representation of principal components.

A principal component can be expressed by one or more existing variables. For example, we may use a single variable vitamin C to differentiate between food items. Because vitamin C is present in vegetables but absent in meat, the resulting plot (leftmost column in Figure 3) will differentiate vegetables from meat, but it will also result in meat items being clumped together.

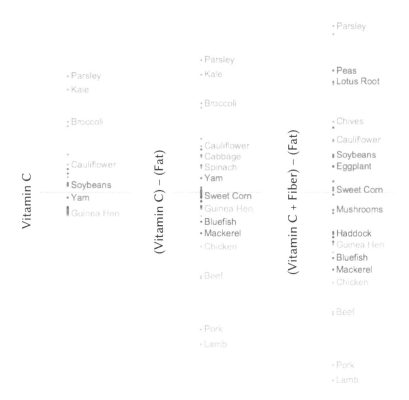

Figure 3. Food items sorted by different combinations of variables.

To spread the meat items out, we can use fat content as a secondary variable, since fat is present in meat but mostly absent in vegetables. However, since fat and vitamin C are measured in different units, we first have to standardize them before they can be combined.

Standardization is analogous to expressing each variable in terms of percentiles, which shifts variables onto a uniform standard scale, thus allowing us to combine them to calculate a new variable:

```
vitamin C - fat
```

As vitamin C spreads the vegetable distribution upward, we minus fat to spread the meats downward. Combining the two variables thus helps to spread out both the vegetable and meat items (center column in Figure 3).

The spread can be further improved by adding fiber, which vegetable items have in varying levels:

```
(vitamin C + fiber) - fat
```

This new variable gives us the best data spread yet (rightmost column in Figure 3).

While we derived principal components for this example by trial-and-error, PCA can do it systematically. We will see how this works in the following example.

3.3 Example: Analyzing Food Groups

Using open data from the *United States Department of Agriculture*, we analyzed the nutritional content of a random sample of food items by considering four nutrition variables: fat, protein, fiber and vitamin C. As shown in Figure 4, we can see that certain nutrients tend to co-exist in food items.

Specifically, levels of fat and protein appear to move in the same direction, and also in the opposite direction from fiber and vitamin C levels. To confirm our guess, we can check whether nutrition variables are correlated (see Chapter 6.5). Indeed, we would find significant positive correlation between fat and protein levels (r = 0.56), as well as between fiber and vitamin C levels (r = 0.57).

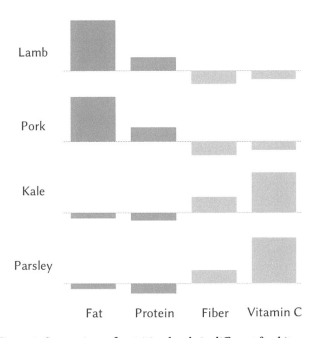

Figure 4. Comparison of nutrition levels in different food items.

Therefore, instead of analyzing the four nutrition variables separately, we can combine highly-correlated variables, hence leaving just two dimensions to consider. This is why PCA is called a *dimension reduction* technique.

When we apply PCA to our food dataset, we get the principal components displayed in Figure 5.

	PC1	PC2	PC3	PC4
Fat	-0.45	0.66	0.58	0.18
Protein	-0.55	0.21	-0.46	-0.67
Fiber	0.55	0.19	0.43	-0.69
Vitamin C	0.44	0.70	-0.52	0.22

Figure 5. Principal components as optimally weighted combinations of nutrition variables. Pink cells within the same principal component represent variables that are weighted in the same direction.

Each principal component is a weighted combination of nutrition variables, where weights can be positive, negative or close to zero. For example, to get the first principal component (PC1) value for a particular food item, we would solve for the following:

```
.55(fiber) + .44(vitamin C) - .45(fat) - .55(protein)
```

So instead of combining variables via trial-and-error as we did previously, PCA computes precise weights with which variables can be combined to best differentiate our items.

Notice that the top principal component (PC1) summarizes our findings so far—fat has been paired with protein, and fiber with vitamin C, and the two pairs are inversely related.

While PC1 differentiates meat from vegetables, the second principal component (PC2) further identifies sub-categories within meat (using fat) and vegetables (using vitamin C). When we use PC1 and PC2 to plot food items, we achieve the best data spread thus far (as shown in Figure 6).

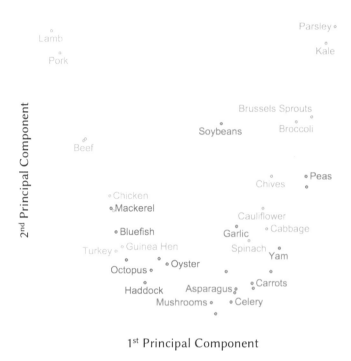

Figure 6. Plot of food items using the top two principal components.

Meat items (labelled in blue) have low PC1 values, and are thus concentrated on the left of the plot, on the opposite side from vegetable items (labelled in orange). We can also see that among the meat items, seafood (labelled in dark blue) have lower fat content, thus they score lower on PC2 and reside at the bottom left corner of the plot. Similarly, several non-leafy vegetarian items (labelled in dark orange) have lower vitamin C content and thus lower PC2 values, as marked at the bottom right corner of the plot.

Choosing the Number of Components. Our example above generated four principal components, corresponding to the original number of variables in the dataset. Since principal components are derived from existing variables, the information available to differentiate between data points is constrained by our original number of variables.

However, to keep results simple and generalizable, we should only select the first few principal components for visualization and further analysis. Principal components are arranged by their effectiveness in differentiating data points, with the first principal component doing so to the largest degree. The number of principal components to shortlist is determined by a *scree plot*, which we had last seen in the last chapter.

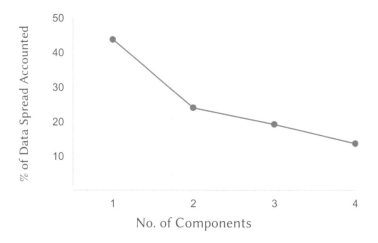

Figure 7. Scree plot showing a 'kink' indicating that the optimal number of principal components is two.

A scree plot shows the decreasing effectiveness of subsequent principal components in differentiating data points (see Figure 7). A rule of thumb is to use the number of principal components corresponding to the location of a *kink*, which is a sharp bend in the scree plot.

In Figure 7, the kink is located at the second component. This means that even though having three or more principal components would better differentiate data points, this extra information may not justify the resulting complexity of the solution. As we can see from the scree plot, the top two principal components already account for about 70% of data spread. Using fewer principal components to explain the current data sample better ensures that the same components can be generalized to a future sample.

3.4 Limitations

PCA is a useful technique for analyzing datasets with many variables. However, it has drawbacks:

Maximizing Spread. PCA makes an important assumption that dimensions with the largest spread of data points are also the most useful. However, this may not be true. A popular counter example is the task of counting pancakes arranged in a stack.

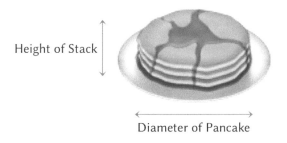

Figure 8. Pancake-counting analogy.

To count the number of pancakes, we differentiate one pancake from the next along the vertical axis (i.e. height of stack). However, if the stack is short, PCA would erroneously identify the horizontal axis (i.e. diameter of pancakes) as the best principal component for our task since it would be the dimension along which there is largest spread.

Interpreting Components. A key challenge with PCA is that interpretations of generated components have to be inferred, and sometimes, we may struggle to explain why variables would be combined in a certain way.

Nonetheless, having prior domain knowledge could help. In our example with food items, prior knowledge of major food categories helped us to understand why nutrition variables were combined the way they were to form principal components.

Orthogonal Components. PCA always generates *orthogonal* principal components, which means that components are positioned at 90 degrees to each other. However, this assumption is restrictive as informative dimensions may not be orthogonal. To resolve this, we can use an alternative technique known as *Independent Component Analysis* (ICA).

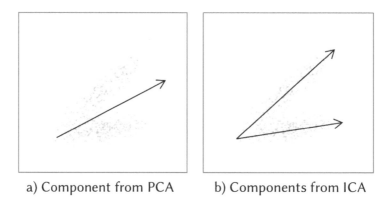

a) Component from PCA   b) Components from ICA

Figure 9. Comparison of how PCA and ICA identify important components.

ICA allows its components to be non-orthogonal, but forbids them to overlap in the information they contain (see Figure 9). This results in each independent component revealing unique information on the dataset. In addition to overcoming the orthogonality assumption, ICA also looks beyond data spread in determining its components, and is hence less susceptible to the pancake error.

While ICA may seem superior, PCA remains one of the most popular techniques for dimension reduction, and knowing how it works will prove useful. When in doubt, you could always consider running an ICA to verify and complement results from a PCA.

3.5 Summary

- Principal Component Analysis (PCA) is known as a *dimension reduction* technique because it allows us to express our data with a smaller set of variables, of which are called *principal components.*
- Each principal component is a weighted sum of original variables. Top principal components can be used to improve analysis and visualization.
- PCA works best when the most informative dimensions have the largest data spread and are orthogonal to each other.

4. Association Rules

4.1 Discovering Purchasing Patterns

When you go grocery shopping, you would bring along a list of things to purchase based on your needs and preferences. A housewife might buy healthy ingredients for a family dinner, while a bachelor might buy beer and chips. Understanding these buying patterns can help to increase sales in several ways. For example, if a pair of items, X and Y, are frequently bought together:

- Advertisements for X could be targeted at buyers of Y
- X and Y could be placed on the same shelf, so buyers of one item would be prompted to buy the other
- X and Y could be combined into a new product, such as having X in flavors of Y

To uncover how items are associated with each other, we can use *association rules*. Besides increasing sales profits, association rules can also be used in other fields. In medical diagnoses, for instance, understanding comorbid symptoms can help to improve patient care.

4.2 Support, Confidence and Lift

There are three common measures used to identify associations.

Measure 1: Support. This indicates *how frequently an itemset appears*, measured by the proportion of transactions in which the itemset is present. In Table 1, {apple} appears in four out of eight transactions, and hence its support is 50%. Itemsets can also contain multiple items—for instance, the support of {apple,beer,rice} is two out of eight, or 25%. A *support threshold* could be chosen to identify frequent itemsets, such that itemsets with support values above this threshold would be deemed as frequent.

$$\text{Support } \{\text{🍎}\} = \frac{4}{8}$$

Figure 1. Support measure.

Transaction 1	🍎 🍺 🍈 🍗
Transaction 2	 🍎 🍺 🍈
Transaction 3	🍎 🍺
Transaction 4	🍎 🍌
Transaction 5	🍼 🍺 🍈 🍗
Transaction 6	🍼 🍺 🍈
Transaction 7	🍼 🍺
Transaction 8	 🍼 🍌

Table 1. Example transactions.

Measure 2: Confidence. This indicates *how frequently item Y would appear if item X is present*, expressed as {X->Y}. This is measured by the proportion of transactions with item X where item Y also appears. Based on Table 1, the confidence of {apple->beer} is three out of four, or 75%.

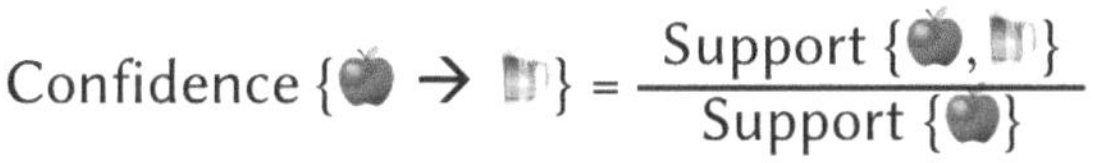

$$\text{Confidence } \{ \text{🍎} \rightarrow \text{🍺} \} = \frac{\text{Support } \{ \text{🍎}, \text{🍺} \}}{\text{Support } \{ \text{🍎} \}}$$

Figure 2. Confidence measure.

One drawback of this measure is that it might misrepresent the importance of an association. The example in Figure 2 only accounts how frequently purchases are made for apples, but not for beers. If beers are also very popular in general, which seems the case in Table 1, then it is obvious that a transaction containing apples will likely also contain beers, thus inflating the confidence measure. However, we can account for the base frequency of both constituent items by using a third measure.

Measure 3: Lift. This indicates *how frequently items X and Y appear together, while accounting for how frequently each would appear on its own.*

Therefore, the lift of {apple->beer} is equal to the confidence of {apple->beer} divided by the frequency of {beer}.

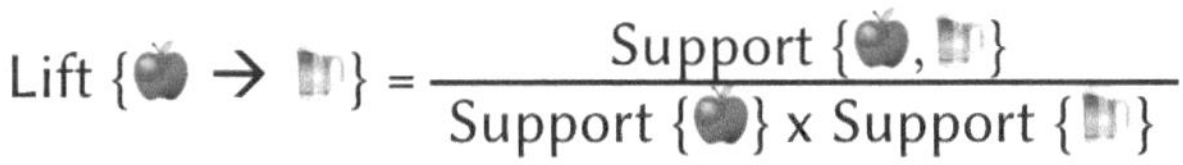

$$\text{Lift } \{ \text{🍎} \rightarrow \text{🍺} \} = \frac{\text{Support } \{ \text{🍎}, \text{🍺} \}}{\text{Support } \{ \text{🍎} \} \times \text{Support } \{ \text{🍺} \}}$$

Figure 3. Lift measure.

Based on Table 1, the lift of {apple->beer} will equal to one, implying no association between the items. A lift value greater than one means that item Y is *likely* to be bought if item X is bought, while a value less than one means that item Y is *unlikely* to be bought if item X is bought.

4.3 Example: Transacting Grocery Sales

To demonstrate the use of association measures, we analyze data collected from a grocery store over 30 days. Figure 4 shows associations between pairs of grocery items with confidence and lift values larger than 0.9% and 2.3 respectively. Bigger circles imply higher support, while red circles imply higher lift.

Figure 4. Network graph of associations between grocery items.

We can observe several purchasing patterns here:

- The most frequent transaction was of pip and tropical fruits
- Another frequent transaction was of onions and vegetables
- One likely bought sausages if they had bought sliced cheese
- One likely bought tropical fruit if they had bought tea

Recall that one drawback of the confidence measure is that it could misrepresent the importance of an association. To demonstrate this, here are three association rules containing beer:

Transaction	Support	Confidence	Lift
Beer → Soda	1.38%	17.8%	1.0
Beer → Berries	0.08%	1.0%	0.3
Beer → Male Cosmetics	0.09%	1.2%	2.6

Table 2. **Association measures for three beer-related rules.**

The {beer->soda} rule had the highest confidence at 17.8%. However, both beer and soda appeared frequently across all transactions (see Table 3), so their association could simply be a coincidence. This is confirmed by their lift value of one, implying no association between purchases of beer and soda.

Transaction	Support
Beer	7.77%
Soda	17.44%
Berries	3.32%
Male Cosmetics	0.46%

Table 3. **Support values of individual items in beer-related rules.**

On the other hand, the {beer->male cosmetics} rule had a low confidence, due to few purchases of male cosmetics in general. Nonetheless, if one had bought male cosmetics, they probably would buy beer as well, which we can infer from the high lift value of 2.6. The converse was true for {beer->berries}. With a lift value below one, we can conclude that if one had bought beer, they probably would not buy berries.

While it is easy to determine the frequency of individual itemsets, a business owner would typically be more interested in obtaining a complete list of popular itemsets that are bought frequently. For this, we need to calculate support values for every possible itemset configuration, before shortlisting those with support values above a chosen threshold.

In a store with just 10 items, the total number of possible configurations to examine would be a whopping 1023 (i.e. 2^{10} - 1), and this number grows exponentially bigger in a store with hundreds of items. It is clear that we need a more efficient solution.

4.4 Apriori Principle

One way to reduce the number of itemset configurations we need to consider is to make use of the *apriori principle*. Simply put, the apriori principle states that if an itemset is infrequent, then any larger itemsets containing it must also be infrequent. This means that if {beer} was found to be infrequent, so too must be {beer,pizza}. In consolidating the list of frequent itemsets, we therefore need not consider {beer,pizza}, nor any other itemset containing beer.

Finding itemsets with high support

Using the apriori principle, we can obtain the list of frequent itemsets in these steps:

Step 0: Start with itemsets containing just a single item, such as {apple} and {pear}.

Step 1: Determine the support for each itemset. Retain itemsets that meet the minimum support threshold, and toss out those that do not.

Step 2: Increase the size of candidate itemsets by one item, and generate all possible configurations using itemsets retained in the previous step.

Step 3: Repeat Steps 1 and 2, determining the support for ever-larger itemsets, until there are no new itemsets to examine.

Figure 5 shows how candidate itemsets can be significantly pruned using the apriori principle. If {apple} had low support, it would be removed along with all other candidate itemsets containing it, hence reducing the number that needs to be examined by more than half.

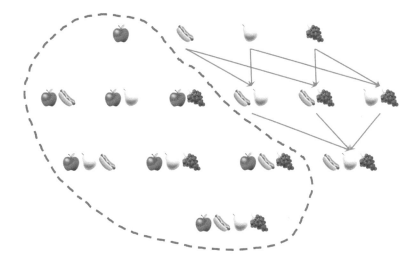

Figure 5. Itemsets within the red border would be pruned.

Finding item rules with high confidence or lift

Apart from identifying itemsets with high support, the apriori principle can also identify item associations with high confidence or lift. Finding these associations is less computationally taxing once high-support itemsets have been identified, since confidence and lift are calculated using support values.

Take for example the task of finding high-confidence rules. If the rule {beer,chips->apple} had low confidence, all other rules with the same constituent items and apple on the right-hand side would have low confidence too, including {beer->apple,chips} and {chips->apple,beer}. As before, these lower level rules can be pruned using the apriori principle, so that fewer candidate rules need to be examined.

4.5 Limitations

Computationally Expensive. Even though the apriori principle reduces the number of candidate itemsets to consider, this number could still be significant if store inventories are large, or when the support threshold is low. An alternative solution would be to reduce the number of comparisons through the use of advanced data structures to sort candidate itemsets more efficiently.

Spurious Associations. Associations could also happen by chance among a large number of items. To ensure that discovered associations are generalizable, they should be validated (see Chapter 1.4).

Despite these limitations, association rules remain an intuitive method to identify patterns in moderately-sized datasets.

4.6 Summary

- Association rules reveal how frequently items appear on their own or in relation to each other.
- There are three common ways to measure association:
    1. *Support* of {X} indicates how frequently item X appears
    2. *Confidence* of {X->Y} indicates how frequently item Y appears when item X is present
    3. *Lift* of {X->Y} indicates how frequently items X and Y appear together, while accounting for how frequently each would appear on its own
- The *apriori principle* accelerates the search for frequent itemsets by pruning away a large proportion of infrequent ones.

5. Social Network Analysis

5.1 Mapping out Relationships

Most of us have multiple social circles, comprising people like relatives, colleagues or schoolmates. To examine how these people relate to each other, such as identifying prominent individuals and how they drive group dynamics, we could use a technique called *Social Network Analysis* (SNA). SNA has potential applications in viral marketing, epidemic modeling, and even team game strategies. However, it is most known for its use in analyzing relationships in social networks, which gave it its name. Figure 1 illustrates an example of how relationships are represented in SNA.

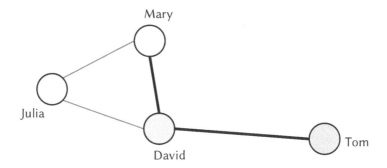

Figure 1. Simple friendship network. Closer friendships are represented by thicker edges.

Figure 1 shows a network, also called a *graph*, of four individuals that are each represented by a *node*. Relationships between nodes are represented by lines, known as *edges*. Each edge can have a *weight*, which indicates the relationship's strength.

From Figure 1, we can tell that:

- David is the most well-connected person, being acquainted with the other three individuals
- Tom does not know anyone else but David, with whom he is good friends
- Julia knows Mary and David, but she is not close to them

Apart from relationships, SNA can also map networks for other entities—as long as they are interconnected. In this chapter, we will use SNA to analyze an international network of weapons trade to discover dominant powers and their spheres of influence.

5.2 Example: Geopolitics in Weapons Trade

We obtained data on bilateral transfers of major conventional weapons from the *Stockholm International Peace Research Institute*. Weapons trade was used as a proxy for bilateral relations as such trade would likely happen only if the countries were aligned on the international stage.

In this analysis, we standardized the value of weapons traded in US dollars with reference to 1990 prices, before taking only trade values above $100 million into consideration. To account for fluctuations in weapons trade due to production cycles of new technology, we looked at the 10-year trade volume from 2006 to 2015 to construct a network of 91 nodes and 295 edges.

Figure 2. Network of countries based on weapons trade.

To visualize the network, a *force-directed algorithm* was used: nodes with no links repel each other, while linked nodes attract each other based on the strength of their connection (see Figure 2). For instance, the largest value of arms traded was between Russia and India ($22.3b), and so the two countries are connected by a thick edge and positioned close together.

By analyzing the resulting network with the Louvain method (explained in the next section), geopolitical alliances were grouped into three clusters:

- **Blue**: This was the largest cluster, dominated by the US and comprising her allies such as the UK and Israel.
- **Yellow**: Led by Germany and comprising mainly European countries, this cluster shared close ties with the blue cluster.
- **Red**: Dominated by Russia and China, this cluster was dissociated from the other two clusters, and comprised mainly Asian and African countries.

The clusters reflected geopolitical realities in the 21st century, such as longstanding alliances among Western nations, polarization between democratic and communist nations, and the growing power struggle between the US and China.

Apart from being grouped into clusters, we also ranked individual countries based on their level of influence using an algorithm known as PageRank (explained later). Figure 3 presents the top 15 most influential countries, which can also be identified by their larger nodes and labels in Figure 2.

Our analysis shows the top five most influential countries to be the US, Russia, Germany, France and China. These results coincide with the fact that four of these countries wield power as permanent members of the *United Nations Security Council.*

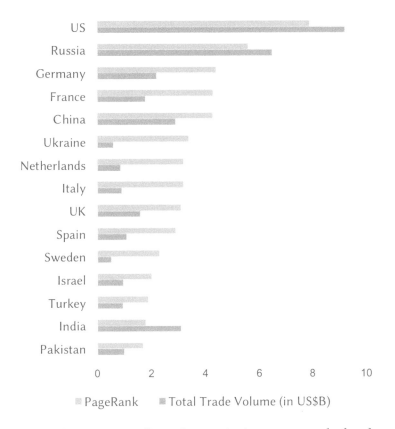

Figure 3. Top 15 most influential countries in weapons trade, based on the PageRank algorithm. Each country's PageRank value (yellow) is shown alongside its total volume of trade (grey).

In the following sections, we will examine the methods that were used to cluster and rank countries.

5.3 Louvain Method

As we saw in Figure 2, we can discover clusters in a network by grouping nodes. Examining these clusters could help us understand how parts of the network differ, and where these differences are bridged.

The *Louvain method* is one way to identify clusters in a network. It experiments with different clustering configurations to 1) maximize the number and strength of edges between nodes in the same cluster, while 2) minimizing those between nodes in different clusters. The degree to which these two conditions are fulfilled is known as *modularity*, and higher modularity indicates more optimal clusters.

To obtain the optimal clustering configuration, the Louvain method iterates through the following steps:

Step 0: Treat each node as a single cluster, such that we start off with as many clusters as there are nodes.

Step 1: Reassign a node into a cluster that results in the highest improvement in modularity. If it is not possible to improve modularity any further, the node stays put. Repeat for every node until there are no more reassignments.

Step 2: Build a coarse-grained version of the network by representing each cluster found in Step 1 as a single node, and consolidating former inter-cluster edges into weighted edges that connect the new nodes.

Step 3: Repeat Steps 1 and 2 until further reassignment and consolidation are not possible.

In this manner, the Louvain method helps us to uncover more significant clusters by first detecting smaller clusters, and then merging them if appropriate. Its simplicity and efficiency makes the Louvain method a popular choice for network clustering. But, it does have its limitations:

Important but small clusters might be subsumed. The iterative merging of clusters could result in important but small clusters being overlooked. To avoid this, we could examine clusters identified in the intermediate iteration phases and retain them if necessary.

Multiple possible clustering configurations. For networks that contain overlapping or nested clusters, it could be difficult to identify the optimal clustering solution. Nonetheless, when there are several solutions with high modularity, we could validate the clusters against other information sources, just as how we compared the clusters in Figure 2 with their similarities in geographical location and political ideology.

5.4 PageRank Algorithm

While clusters reveal regions of highly concentrated interactions, these interactions could be governed by dominant nodes around which clusters form. To identify these dominant nodes, we can use node ranking.

The *PageRank* algorithm, named after Google's co-founder Larry Page, was one of the first algorithms Google used to rank websites. While we describe PageRank here in its most famous context of website ranking, it could be used to rank nodes of any kind.

A website's PageRank is determined by three factors:

- **Number of Links**. If a website is linked to by other websites, it is likely to attract more users.
- **Strength of Links**. The more frequently these links are accessed, the higher the website's traffic.
- **Source of Links**. Being linked to by other high-ranking websites also boosts a website's own rank.

To see how PageRank works, check out the example network in Figure 4, where nodes represent websites and edges are hyperlinks.

An incoming hyperlink of heavier weight implies higher traffic flow toward the website. We see from Figure 4 that a user at website M is twice as likely to visit website D than he is to visit website J, and that he would never visit website T.

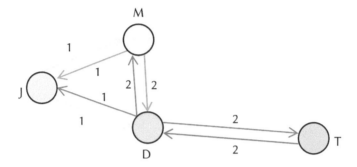

Figure 4. A network where nodes are websites and edges are hyperlinks.

To understand which website attracts the most users, we could simulate the website surfing behavior indicated in Figure 4 for 100 users, and observe which website they eventually land on.

First, we distribute the 100 users equally across the four websites, as shown in Figure 5.

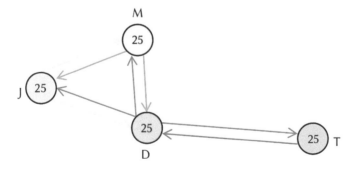

Figure 5. Initial set-up where 100 users are distributed across four websites.

We then redistribute the users out of each website according to the strength of its outgoing links. For example, two-thirds of the users in website M would go to website D, while the remaining one-third visits website J. The edges in Figure 6 show the number of users entering and leaving each website.

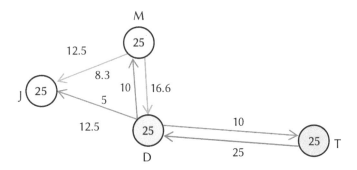

Figure 6. Redistribution of users based on the strength of outgoing links.

After redistributing the users, website M would have about 23 users, of which 10 would be directed from website D and 13 from website J. Figure 7 shows the resulting user distribution at each website, rounded to the nearest integer.

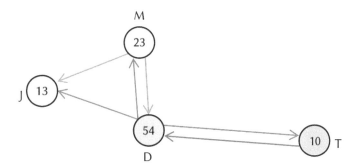

Figure 7. Number of users on each website after redistribution.

To obtain the PageRank of each website, we repeat this user redistribution process until there are no further changes to the number of users on each website. The final number of users on each website would then correspond to its PageRank—the more users it attracts, the higher its rank.

We could also measure a country's dominance with PageRank in much the same way. In a weapons trade network, a country of high PageRank would be one that engages in many high-value trade deals with other high-ranking countries—hence making it an influential player with a high degree of centrality in the global weapons trade network.

Despite its ease of use, the PageRank algorithm does have a limitation: it is **biased toward older nodes**. For example, while a new webpage could contain excellent content, its relative obscurity in the beginning would earn it a low PageRank, and potentially cause it to be dismissed from site recommendations. To prevent this, PageRank values could be updated regularly to give new websites a chance to rise up the ranks as they build their reputations.

This bias is not always detrimental, however, especially when ranking entities that build influence over longer timelines—say, for when we are interested in ranking countries based on dominance. This shows that an algorithm's limitation could potentially work in one's favor, depending on the research question.

5.5 Limitations

While clustering and ranking methods allow us to gain deeper insights into a network, the results should be interpreted with care.

Take for example our use of weapons trade data to assess countries' relations. This simplistic measure has several pitfalls:

Overlooking diplomatic relations if no weapon trade took place. Most edges only form between weapon exporters and importers.

Hence, friendly relations between two countries which are both weapon importers (or exporters) would not be reflected.

Omitting other considerations in weapon sales. Weapons may need to be integrated with existing legacy systems, hence limiting potential purchases. In addition, exporting countries may prioritize domestic considerations (e.g. economic benefits) over bilateral relations in making decisions on weapon sales. This could explain why Ukraine, a significant weapon exporter, was ranked 6th despite a lack of reputation as an influential country.

Since the validity of our conclusions depends on how well the data represents the construct we are attempting to measure, the type of data used to generate the network must be carefully selected. To verify that the chosen data sources are viable and analysis techniques sufficiently robust, we should check results against other sources of information.

5.6 Summary

- Social network analysis is a technique that allows us to map and analyze relationships between entities.
- The *Louvain method* identifies clusters in a network in a way that maximizes interactions within clusters and minimizes those between clusters. It works best when clusters are equally sized and discrete.
- The *PageRank* algorithm ranks nodes in a network based on their number of links, as well as the strength and source of those links. While this helps us to identify dominant nodes in a network, it is also biased against newer nodes, which would have had less time to build up substantial links.

6. Regression Analysis

6.1 Deriving a Trend Line

Trend lines are a popular tool for predictions because they are easy to generate and understand. You only need to flip through your daily newspaper to see trend charts for topics ranging from stock prices to temperature forecast, and everything in between.

Common trends typically involve a single predictor used to predict an outcome, such as using time (predictor) to predict the price of a company's stock (outcome). However, we could improve predictions by adding more predictors, such as using sales revenue in addition to time to predict stock price.

This can be done with *regression analysis*, which allows us not only to improve predictions by accounting for multiple predictors, but also to compare the strength of each predictor.

To see how this is done, let us look at a case study on predicting house prices.

6.2 Example: Predicting House Prices

We used data on house prices in Boston and their related predictors during the 1970s. Based on a preliminary analysis, the two strongest predictors of house prices were the number of rooms in the house, and the proportion of residents in the neighborhood with low income.

From Figure 1, we can see that expensive houses generally have more rooms. To predict the price of a house, we could draw a trend line (in blue), also known as a *best-fit line*, that passes through or sits close to as many data points in the plot as possible. For example, if a house had eight rooms, it would cost approximately $38,150.

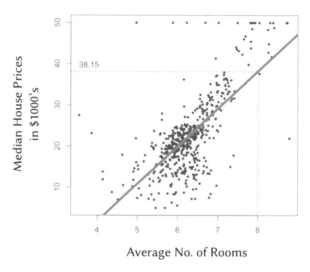

Figure 1. House price against number of rooms.

Apart from the number of rooms, the price of a house was also affected by its neighborhood. Houses were cheaper where there were higher proportions of low income residents (see Figure 2). As the trend was slightly curved (Figure 2a), we applied a mathematical transformation known as the logarithm to the predictor values so that the data points could be better represented by a straight trend line (Figure 2b).

We can observe that data points were more concentrated along the trend line in Figure 2b than in Figure 1, implying that neighborhood affluence was a stronger predictor of house price than number of rooms.

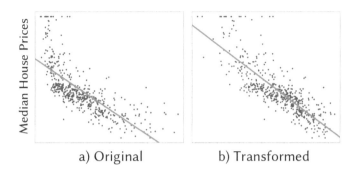

a) Original   b) Transformed

Figure 2. House price against proportion of neighborhood with low income.

To improve house price estimates, we could use a combination of number of rooms and neighborhood affluence as predictors. However, since neighborhood affluence has been found to be a stronger predictor than number of rooms, simply summing up both predictors would not be ideal. Instead, predictions using neighborhood affluence should be given a heavier weight.

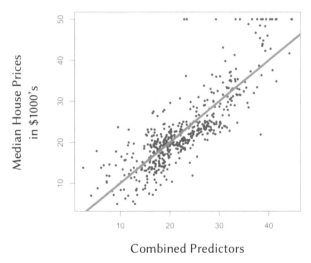

Combined Predictors

Figure 3. House price against a weighted combination of number of rooms and neighborhood affluence.

Figure 3 shows house prices plotted against an optimally weighted combination of the two predictors. Notice that data points lie even closer to the resulting trend line than before, so predictions made using this trend line would likely be the most accurate. To verify this, we could compare average prediction errors from using the three trend lines we have seen thus far (see Table 1).

	Prediction Error (in $1000's)
No. of Rooms	4.4
Neighborhood Affluence	3.9
No. of Rooms & Neighborhood Affluence	3.7

Table 1. Average prediction errors from using the three trend lines.

While it is clear that a weighted combination of predictors would lead to more accurate predictions, there leaves two questions to be answered: 1) how do we derive the optimal set of weights and 2) how should we interpret them?

6.3 Gradient Descent

Predictor weights are the main parameters in a regression analysis, and optimal weights are usually derived directly by solving equations. However, since regression analysis is simple and apt for illustrating concepts, we will use it to explain an alternative method for optimizing parameters. This method is called gradient descent, and is used when parameters cannot be derived directly.

In a nutshell, the *gradient descent* algorithm makes an initial guess on a set of suitable weights, before starting an iterative process of applying these weights to every data point to make predictions, and then tweaking these weights in order to reduce overall prediction error.

This process can be likened to taking steps to reach the bottom of a hill. At each step, the gradient descent algorithm determines which direction provides the steepest descent, and re-calibrates the weights toward that direction. Eventually, we will reach the lowest point—which is also the point where prediction error is minimized. Figure 4 illustrates how an optimized regression trend line corresponds to the lowest point on a gradient.

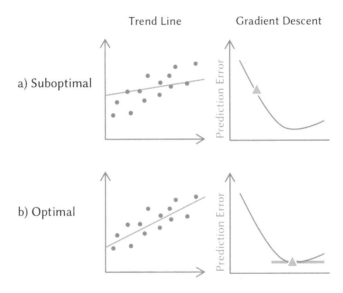

Figure 4. How a trend line approaches optimality via gradient descent.

Besides regression, gradient descent can also be used to optimize parameters in other models such as support vector machines (see Chapter 8) and neural networks (see Chapter 11). In these more complex models, however, the results of gradient descent could be affected by where we start off on the hill (i.e. initial parameter values). For example, if we happen to start just above a small pit, the gradient descent algorithm might mistake that as the optimal point (see Figure 5).

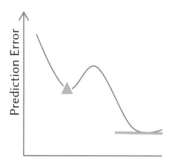

Figure 5. How a nearby pit could be mistaken as the optimal point (green triangle), when the true optimum is further below (green horizontal line).

To reduce the risk of getting stuck in a pit, we could instead use *stochastic gradient descent*, where rather than using *every* data point to adjust parameters in each iteration, we reference only *one*. This introduces variability, which could allow the algorithm to escape from a pit. While the resulting parameter values from the stochastic process might not be precisely optimal, they are usually close enough to yield decent accuracy.

Nonetheless, this potential 'pitfall' applies only to more complex models, and we need not worry about it when conducting regression analysis.

6.4 Regression Coefficients

After deriving the best set of weights for our regression predictors, we need to interpret them.

Weights of regression predictors are formally called *regression coefficients*. A predictor's regression coefficient measures *how strong that predictor is, in the presence of other predictors*. In other words, it is the *value added* by that predictor, rather than its absolute predictive strength.

For example, if we had used the floor area of a house along with its number of rooms to predict a house's price, the weight for number of rooms might turn out to be negligible. Since the number of rooms overlaps with floor area in measuring the size of a house, it adds little value to overall predictive power.

Predictors measured in different units would also interfere with our interpretation of regression coefficients. For example, a predictor measured in centimeters would have a weight that is 100 times smaller than the same one measured in meters. To avoid this, we should *standardize* the units of predictor variables before conducting a regression analysis. Standardization is analogous to expressing each variable in terms of percentiles. When predictors have been standardized, their coefficients would be called *beta weights*, which could be used for more accurate comparisons.

In our housing price example, the two predictors of 1) number of rooms and 2) proportion of low income neighborhood residents were both standardized and weighted in a ratio of 2.7 to 6.3. This means that the proportion of low income residents was a much stronger predictor for house price compared to number of rooms. The regression equation would look something like:

```
price = 2.7(no. of rooms) - 6.3(% of low income residents)
```

In this equation, notice that the proportion of low income residents has a negative weight, as represented by the minus sign. This is because the predictor was negatively associated with house prices, as shown by the downward-sloping trend lines in Figure 2.

6.5 Correlation Coefficients

When there is only one predictor, the beta weight of that predictor is called a *correlation coefficient*, denoted as *r*. Correlation coefficients range from -1 to 1, and provide two pieces of information:

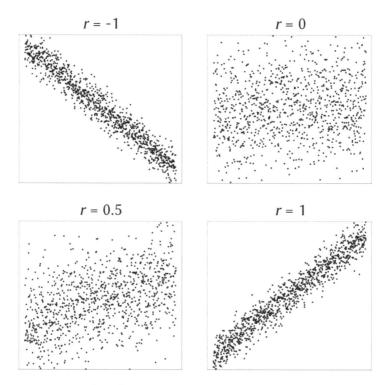

Figure 6. Examples of data spread corresponding to various correlation coefficients.

Direction. Positive coefficients imply that the predictor moves in the same direction as the outcome; negative coefficients indicate the opposite. The price of a house is positively correlated with its number of rooms, but negatively correlated with the proportion of low income residents in the neighborhood.

Magnitude. The closer the coefficient is to -1 or 1, the stronger the predictor. For example, the correlation coefficient denoted by the trend line in Figure 1 is 0.7, while that in Figure 2b is -0.8. This means that neighborhood affluence is a stronger predictor of a house's price than its number of rooms. A correlation of zero would imply no relation between a predictor and the outcome. Since correlation coefficients indicate the absolute strength of individual predictors, they are a more reliable method of ranking predictors than regression coefficients.

6.6 Limitations

While informative and fast to compute, regression analysis has its drawbacks:

Sensitivity to Outliers. As regression analysis accounts for all data points equally, having just a few data points with extreme values could skew the trend line significantly. To detect this, we could use scatterplots to identify outliers before further analysis.

Distorted Weights of Correlated Predictors. The inclusion of highly-correlated predictors in a regression model would distort the interpretation of their weights, resulting in a problem known as *multicollinearity*. To overcome multicollinearity, we could either exclude correlated predictors prior to analysis, or use more advanced techniques such as *lasso* or *ridge* regression.

Curved Trends. In our example, trends were depicted with a straight line. However, some trends might be curved, such as in Figure 2a, and we might need to transform the predictor values or use alternative algorithms such as support vector machines (see Chapter 8).

Does Not Imply Causation. Suppose that dog ownership was found to be positively correlated with house prices. We know that adopting a pet dog would not increase the value of your house—but rather, households that can afford to own dogs tend to have higher income, and likely live in affluent neighborhoods where houses tend to fetch higher prices.

Despite these limitations, regression analysis remains one of the most common, easy-to-use and intuitive techniques for making predictions. Being mindful of how we interpret results will help to ensure the accuracy of our conclusions.

6.7 Summary

- Regression analysis finds the best-fit trend line that passes through or sits close to as many data points as possible.
- A trend line is derived from a weighted combination of predictors. The weights are called *regression coefficients*, which indicate the strength of a predictor in the presence of other predictors.
- Regression analysis works best when there is little correlation between predictors, no outliers, and when the expected trend is a straight line.

7. k-Nearest Neighbors and Anomaly Detection

7.1 Food Forensics

Let's talk about wine. Have you ever wondered about the real differences between red and white wine?

Some simply assume that red wine is made from red grapes, and white wine from white grapes. But this is not entirely true, because white wine can also be made from red grapes, although red wine cannot be made from white grapes.

The key difference lies in the way the grapes are fermented. For red wine, grape juice is fermented together with grape skins, which exude the distinctive red pigments, while white wine is fermented juice without the skin.

Although we may visually infer the presence of grape skins by the wine's color, they do manifest in changes to the wine's chemical makeup. This means that without looking at the wine, we could potentially deduce its color based on the levels of its chemical compounds.

To check this hypothesis, we can use one of the simplest methods in machine learning—a technique known as k-Nearest Neighbors.

7.2 Birds of a Feather Flock Together

k-Nearest Neighbors (*k*-NN) is an algorithm that classifies a data point based on the classification of its neighbors. This means that if a data point is surrounded by four red points and one black point, then majority vote would suggest that the data point is likely red.

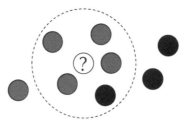

Figure 1. The center data point would be classified as red by a majority vote from its five nearest neighbors.

The *k* in *k*-NN is a parameter referring to the number of nearest neighbors to include in the majority voting process. In the example above, *k* equals to five. Choosing the right value of *k* is a process known as parameter tuning, and is critical to prediction accuracy.

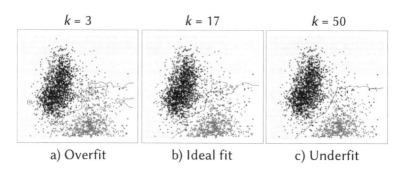

Figure 2. Comparison of model fit using varying values of k. Points in the black region are predicted to be white wines, while those in the red region are predicted to be red wines.

If k is too small (Figure 2a), data points would match only its immediate neighbors and amplify errors due to random noise. If k is too large (Figure 2c), data points would try to match far-flung neighbors, diluting the underlying patterns. But when k is just right (Figure 2b), data points would reference a suitable number of neighbors such that errors cancel each other out to reveal subtle trends in the data.

To achieve the best fit and lowest error, the parameter k can be tuned by cross-validation (see Chapter 1.4). In a binary (i.e. two-class) classification problem, we can also avoid tied votes by choosing k to be an odd number.

Apart from classifying data points into groups, k-NN can also be used to predict continuous values by aggregating the values of nearest neighbors. Instead of treating all neighbors as equal and taking a simple average, the estimate could be improved by using a weighted average: the values of closer neighbors, being more likely to reflect a data point's true value, would be weighted heavier than those further away.

7.3 Example: Distilling Differences in Wine

Going back to our wine example—it would be possible to guess the color of a particular wine by referring to the color of neighboring wines with similar chemical makeup.

Using data on red and white variants of Portuguese *Vinho Verde* wine, we plotted the chemical makeup of 1599 red and 4898 white wines by using two chemical compounds—chlorides and sulfur dioxide—as the axes (see Figure 3).

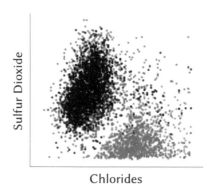

Figure 3. Levels of chlorides and sulfur dioxide in white wines (in black) and red wines (in red).

As grape skins contain a higher concentration of minerals such as sodium chloride (the same compound present in table salt), we will notice a higher infusion of these in red wines. Grape skin also contains natural anti-oxidants that keep the fruit fresh. Without these, white wines require more sulfur dioxide, which acts as a preservative. For these reasons, Figure 3 shows clustering of the red wines at the bottom-right of the plot, and white wines at the top-left.

To deduce the color of a wine with specified levels of chlorides and sulfur dioxide, we can refer to the known colors of neighboring wines with similar quantities of both chemical compounds. By doing this for each point in the plot, we can draw boundaries that distinguish red wines from white (see Figure 2). With an ideal fit (Figure 2b), we can predict a wine's color with over 98% accuracy.

7.4 Anomaly Detection

k-NN is not limited merely to predicting groups or values of data points. It can also be used to identify anomalies, such as in fraud detection. Moreover, the process of identifying anomalies could lead to additional insights, such as discovering a predictor that was previously overlooked.

Anomaly detection is simplest when the data can be visualized. In Figure 3, for instance, we can immediately see which wines deviate from their clusters. However, it may not always be feasible to visualize data on 2-dimensional plots, especially when there are more than two predictor variables to examine. This is where predictive models such as k-NN come in.

As k-NN uses underlying patterns in the data to make predictions, prediction errors are thus telltale signs of data points that do not conform to overall trends. In fact, this approach means that any algorithm that generates a predictive model could be used to detect anomalies. For instance, in regression analysis (Chapter 6), an anomalous point could be easily identified as one that deviates significantly from the best-fit line.

If we reviewed our wine data for anomalies (i.e. color misclassifications), we would discover that red wines that get misclassified as white wines tend to have higher-than-usual sulfur dioxide content. If we had known that these wines required more sulfur dioxide preservatives due to their lower acidity levels, we might consider accounting for wine acidity to improve predictions.

While anomalies could be caused by missing predictors, they could also arise from a lack of sufficient data to train the predictive model. The fewer data points we have, the more difficult it would be to discern patterns in the data, which makes it important for us to ensure an adequate sample size for modeling.

Once anomalies have been identified, they can be removed from the dataset before training the predictive model. This will reduce noise in the data, and strengthen the accuracy of the model.

7.5 Limitations

Although *k*-NN is simple and effective, we should be aware that there are scenarios for which it might not perform well:

Imbalanced Classes. If there are multiple classes to be predicted, and the classes differ drastically in size, data points belonging to the smallest class might be overshadowed by those from larger classes and suffer from higher risk of misclassification. To improve accuracy, we could use weighted voting instead of majority voting, which would ensure that the classes of closer neighbors are weighted more heavily than those further away.

Excess Predictors. If there are too many predictors to consider, it would be computationally intensive to identify and process nearest neighbors across multiple dimensions. Moreover, some predictors may be redundant and do not improve prediction accuracy. To resolve this, we can use dimension reduction (see Chapter 3) to extract only the most powerful predictors for analysis.

7.6 Summary

- The *k*-Nearest Neighbors (*k*-NN) technique classifies a data point by referencing the classifications of other data points it is closest to.
- *k* is the number of data points to reference, and is determined via *cross-validation*.
- *k*-NN works best when predictors are few and classes are about the same size. Inaccurate classifications could nonetheless be flagged as potential anomalies.

8. Support Vector Machine

8.1 "*No*" or "*Oh No*"?

Medical diagnosis is complex. There may be multiple symptoms to be accounted for, and the process may be vulnerable to the subjective opinions of doctors. Sometimes, the correct diagnosis is not made until it is too late. A more systematic approach to diagnosing underlying ailments might be to use algorithms trained on entire medical databases to generate more accurate predictions.

In this chapter, we will examine a prediction technique known as *support vector machine* (SVM) that derives an optimal classification boundary, which can be used to separate patients into two groups (e.g. healthy vs. unhealthy).

8.2 Example: Predicting Heart Disease

Heart disease is one of the most common health conditions in developed countries, involving the narrowing or blocking of heart vessels that leads to increased risk of heart attack. The condition can be diagnosed conclusively with an imaging scan, but the costs of these scans prohibit most people from undergoing them regularly. An alternative solution would be to shortlist high risk patients, based on physiological symptoms, who would benefit most from regular scanning.

To determine which symptoms predict the presence of heart disease, patients from an American clinic were asked to exercise while their physiological states were recorded, including indicators such as one's maximum heart rate reached during exercise. Subsequently, imaging scans were performed to determine the presence of heart disease. By developing an SVM prediction model that considered heart rate data together with the patient's age, we were able to predict—with over 75% accuracy—if someone was suffering from heart disease.

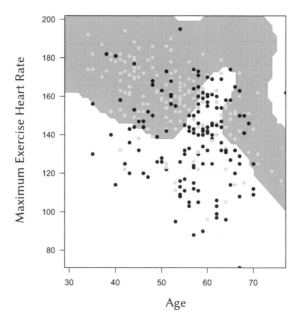

Figure 1. Using SVM to predict the presence of heart disease. The dark green region represents the profile of healthy adults, while the gray region represents the profile of heart disease patients. The light green and black points represent healthy adults and heart disease patients respectively.

In general, patients with heart disease (in black) had lower heart rates during exercise as compared to healthy adults (in light green) of the same age, and the disease appeared to be more prevalent among those older than 55 years.

While heart rate appears to decrease with age, heart disease patients who were about 60 years old actually showed faster heart rates similar to those of younger healthy adults, as indicated by the abrupt arc in the decision boundary. If not for SVM's ability to pick up curved patterns, we might have overlooked this phenomenon.

8.3 Delineating an Optimal Boundary

The main objective of SVM is to derive an optimal boundary that separates one group from another. This is not as simple as it sounds, given that there are numerous possibilities (see Figure 2).

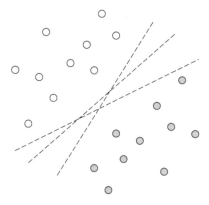

Figure 2. Multiple ways to separate two groups.

To find the optimal boundary, we need to first identify peripheral data points that are located closest to points from the other group. The optimal boundary is then drawn down the middle between peripheral data points of both groups (see Figure 3). As these peripheral data points support the discovery of the optimal boundary, they are also known as *support vectors*.

One advantage of SVM is its computational speed. As the decision boundary is determined only by peripheral data points, less time is required for derivation, in contrast to techniques such as regression (see Chapter 6) that account for every data point in determining a trend line.

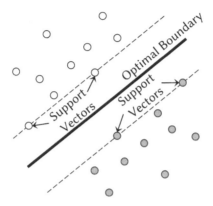

Figure 3. Optimal boundary is located in the middle of peripheral data points from opposing groups.

However, this reliance on a subset of data points also presents a pitfall as the decision boundary therefore becomes more sensitive to the positions of support vectors—and these vary depending on the data points sampled as training data. Furthermore, it is rare for data points to be separated cleanly into groups as shown in Figures 2 and 3. In reality, data points from either group are likely to overlap, as seen in Figure 1.

To overcome these problems, the SVM algorithm has one key feature, a buffer zone, that allows a limited number of training data points to cross over to the incorrect side. This results in a 'softer' boundary that is more robust against outliers, and hence more generalizable to new data.

The buffer zone is created by tuning a *cost parameter* that determines the degree of tolerance for classification errors. A larger cost parameter would increase the tolerance level and result in a wider buffer zone. To ensure that the resulting model yields accurate predictions for current as well as new data, we can determine the best value for the cost parameter via cross-validation (see Chapter 1.4).

Yet another strength of SVM lies in its ability to account for curved patterns in the data. While there are numerous other techniques that could do this, SVM is favored for its superior computational efficiency in deriving intricately curved patterns through a method called the *kernel trick*.

Instead of drawing the curved boundary directly onto the data plane, SVM first projects the data onto a higher dimension for which data points can be separated with a straight line (see Figure 4). These straight lines are simpler to compute, and are also easily translated into curved lines when projected back down onto a lower dimension.

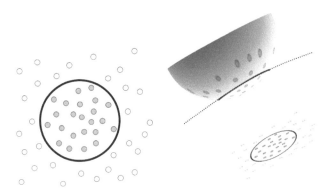

Figure 4. A circle of blue points on a 2-dimensional sheet could be delineated using a straight line when projected onto a 3-dimensional sphere.

SVM's ability to manipulate data in higher dimensions contributes to its popularity in the analysis of datasets with many variables. Its common applications include decoding genetic information and evaluating sentiments in text.

8.4 Limitations

Although SVM is a versatile and fast prediction tool, it might not work well in certain scenarios:

Small Datasets. As SVM relies on support vectors to determine decision boundaries, a small sample would mean fewer of these for accurate positioning of the boundaries.

Multiple Groups. SVM is only able to classify two groups at a time. If there are more than two groups, SVM would need to be iterated to distinguish each group from the rest through a technique known as *multi-class SVM*.

Large Overlap Between Groups. SVM classifies a data point based on which side of the decision boundary it falls on. When a large overlap exists between data points from both groups, a data point near the boundary might be more prone to misclassification. Moreover, SVM does not provide additional information on the probability of misclassification for each data point. We could nonetheless use a data point's distance from the decision boundary to gauge the likelihood of its classification accuracy.

8.5 Summary

- Support Vector Machine (SVM) classifies data points into two groups by drawing a boundary down the middle between peripheral data points (i.e. *support vectors*) of both groups.
- SVM is resilient against outliers as it uses a *buffer zone* that allows a few data points to be on the incorrect side of the boundary. It also employs the *kernel trick* to efficiently derive curved boundaries.
- SVM works best when data points from a large sample have to be classified into two distinct groups.

9. Decision Tree

9.1 Predicting Survival in a Disaster

In a disaster, certain groups of people—such as women and children—might be provided assistance first, hence granting them higher chances of survival. In such situations, we could use *decision trees* to determine the survival of various groups.

A decision tree would predict chance of survival through a series of binary questions (see Figure 1), such that each question has only two possible responses (e.g. 'yes' or 'no'). You would start at the top question, also known as the root node, and move through the tree branches as guided by your responses, until you finally reach a leaf node that indicates your predicted chance of survival.

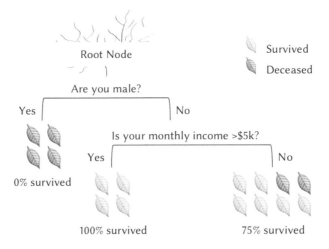

Figure 1. Example decision tree.

9.2 Example: Escaping from the Titanic

To illustrate the use of decision trees in estimating survivability, we used passenger data compiled by the *British Board of Trade* for the ill-fated cruise liner, the *Titanic*, to check which groups of passengers were more likely to have survived. Figure 2 illustrates the decision tree computed to predict passengers' survival rates.

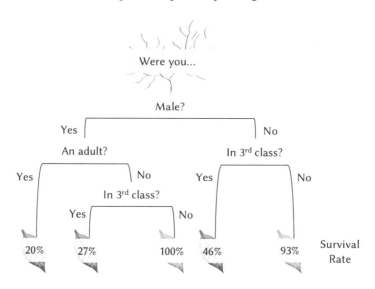

Figure 2. Decision tree predicting if one would survive the sinking of Titanic.

You could easily observe from the tree that you would have had a good chance of being rescued from the *Titanic* if you were either a male child or a female who was not residing in a 3rd class cabin.

Decision trees are incredibly versatile, with broader applications that include predicting survival rates for medical diagnosis, identifying potential staff resignations or detecting fraudulent transactions. They can also handle questions about categorical groupings (e.g. male vs. female) or about continuous values (e.g. income). Note that continuous values could also be represented as groups—for instance, comparing values that are above average against those below average.

In standard decision trees, there are only two possible responses at each branch, such as 'yes' or 'no'. If we wanted to test three or more responses (e.g. 'yes', 'no', 'sometimes'), we could simply add more branches further down the tree (see Figure 3).

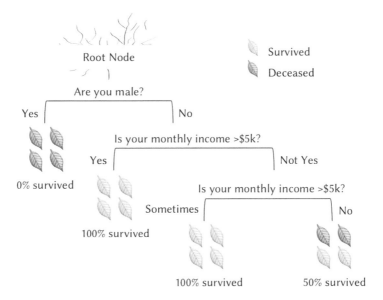

Figure 3. Testing multiple categories in a decision tree.

Decision trees are popular because they are easy to interpret. The question is, how do we generate one?

9.3 Generating a Decision Tree

A decision tree is grown by first splitting all data points into two groups, such that similar data points are grouped together, and then further repeating this binary splitting process within each group. As a result, each subsequent leaf node would have fewer but more homogeneous data points. The basis of decision trees is that data points following the same path are likely to be similar to each other.

The process of repeatedly splitting data to obtain homogeneous groups is called *recursive partitioning*. It involves just two steps:

Step 1: Identify the binary question that best splits data points into two groups that are most homogeneous.

Step 2: Repeat Step 1 for each leaf node, until a stopping criterion is reached.

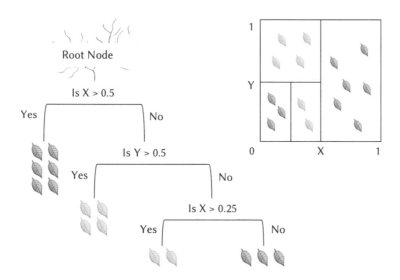

Figure 4. Partitioning of data points by a decision tree visualized in a scatterplot.

There are various possibilities for stopping criteria, which can be selected via cross-validation (see Chapter 1.4). These include:

- Stop when data points at each leaf are all of the same predicted category or value
- Stop when the leaf contains less than five data points
- Stop when further branching does not improve homogeneity beyond a minimum threshold

As recursive partitioning uses only the best binary questions to grow a decision tree, the presence of non-significant variables would not affect results. Moreover, binary questions tend to divide data points around central values, so decision trees are robust against outliers.

9.4 Limitations

While easy to interpret, decision trees do have some drawbacks:

Instability. As decision trees are grown by splitting data points into homogeneous groups, a slight change in the data could trigger changes to the split, and result in a different tree. As decision trees also aim for the best way to split data points each time, they are vulnerable to overfitting (see Chapter 1.3).

Inaccuracy. Using the best binary question to split the data at the start might not lead to the most accurate predictions. Sometimes, less effective splits used initially may lead to better predictions subsequently.

To overcome these limitations, we could avoid aiming for the best split each time and diversify the trees we grow. By later combining predictions from different trees, we could obtain results with better stability and accuracy.

There are two methods to diversifying trees:

- The first method chooses different combinations of binary questions at random to grow multiple trees, and then aggregates the predictions from those trees. This technique is known as building a *random forest* (see Chapter 10).
- Instead of choosing binary questions at random, the second method strategically selects binary questions, such that prediction accuracy for each subsequent tree improves incrementally. A weighted average of predictions from all trees is then taken to obtain the result. This technique is known as *gradient boosting*.

While the random forest and gradient boosting approaches tend to produce more accurate predictions, their complexity renders the solution harder to visualize, hence giving them the moniker of *black-boxes*. This explains why decision trees are still a popular tool for analysis, as their easy visualization lend to simpler assessments of predictors and their interactions.

9.5 Summary

- A decision tree makes predictions by asking a sequence of binary questions.
- The data sample is split repeatedly to obtain homogeneous groups in a process called *recursive partitioning*, until a stopping criterion is reached.
- While easy to use and understand, decision trees are prone to *overfitting*, which leads to inconsistent results. To minimize this, we could use alternative techniques such as *random forests*.

10. Random Forests

10.1 Wisdom of the Crowd

Can several wrongs make a right?

Yes!

While counter-intuitive, this is possible—even expected—for some of the best prediction models.

This plays on the fact that while there are many possible wrong predictions, only one will be correct. By combining models of different strengths and weaknesses, those that yield accurate predictions tend to reinforce each other, while wrong predictions cancel out. This method of combining models to improve prediction accuracy is known as *ensembling*.

We observe this effect in a *random forest*, which is an ensemble of decision trees (see Chapter 9). To show how a random forest is superior to its constituent trees, we generated 1000 possible decision trees to each predict crime in a US city, before comparing their prediction accuracy to that of a random forest grown from the same 1000 trees.

10.2 Example: Forecasting Crime

Open data from the *San Francisco Police Department* provided us with information on the location, date, and severity of crimes that occurred in the city from 2014 to 2016. As research has shown that crimes tend to occur on hotter days, we also obtained the city's weather records for daily temperature and precipitation levels over the same period.

We hypothesized that it would not be feasible for the police force to implement extra security patrols for all areas predicted to have crime, given personnel and resource constraints. As such, we programmed our prediction model to identify only the top 30% of regions with the highest probability of violent crime occurring each day, so that these areas could be prioritized for extra patrols.

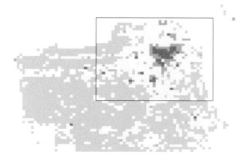

Figure 1. Heat map of San Francisco, showing frequency of crimes: very low (gray), low (yellow), moderate (orange), or high (red).

A preliminary analysis showed that crime occurred mainly in the north-eastern part of the city (as boxed up in Figure 1), and hence we divided it into smaller regions measuring 900ft by 700ft (260m by 220m) for further analysis.

To predict when and where a crime might occur, 1000 possible decision trees were generated based on crime and weather data, before combining them in a random forest. We used the data from 2014 to 2015 to train the prediction models, and tested their accuracy with data from 2016 (January to August).

So how well could we predict crime?

The random forest model successfully predicted 72% (almost three quarters) of all violent crimes. This proved superior to the average prediction accuracy of its 1000 constituent decision trees, which was 67% (see Figure 2).

With only 12 out of 1000 individual trees yielding accuracies better than that from the random forest, we could be 99% certain that predictions from a random forest would be better than those from an individual decision tree.

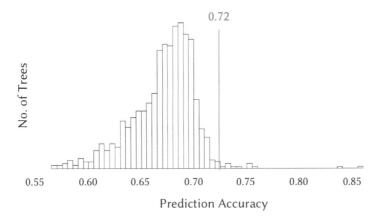

Figure 2. Histogram of prediction accuracies from 1000 decision trees (67% on average), compared to that from combining these trees into a random forest (72%).

Figure 3 shows a sample of the random forest's predictions over four days. Based on our predictions, the police should allocate more resources to areas coded red, and fewer to those coded gray. While it seems obvious that more patrols are required in areas with historically high crime, the model goes further and pinpoints the likelihood of crime in non-red areas. For instance, on Day 4 (lower-right chart), a crime in a gray area was correctly predicted, despite a lack of violent crimes occurring there in the previous three days.

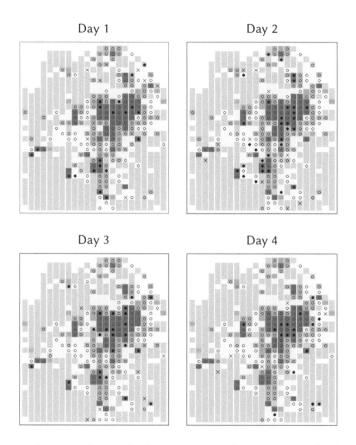

Figure 3. Crime predictions for four consecutive days in 2016. Circles denote locations where a violent crime was predicted to occur. Solid circles denote correct predictions. Crosses denote locations where a violent crime occurred, but was not predicted.

A random forest model also allows us to see which variables contributed most to its predictive accuracy. Based on the chart in Figure 4, crime appears to be best forecasted using crime frequency, location, day of the year and temperatures during the day.

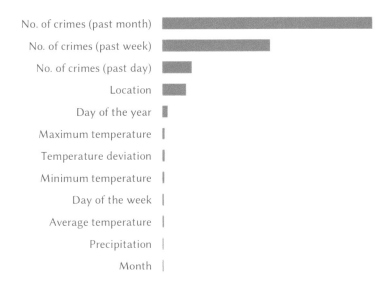

Figure 4. **Top variables contributing to the random forest's accuracy in predicting crime.**

We have seen how effective a random forest could be in predicting complex phenomenon such as crime. But how do they work?

10.3 Ensembles

A random forest is an *ensemble* of decision trees. An ensemble is the term for a prediction model generated by combining predictions from many different models, such as by majority voting or by taking averages.

We show in Figure 5 how an ensemble formed by majority voting could yield more accurate predictions than the individual models it was based on. This is because correct predictions reinforce each other, while errors cancel each other out. But for this effect to work, models included in the ensemble must not make the same kind of errors. In other words, the models must be uncorrelated.

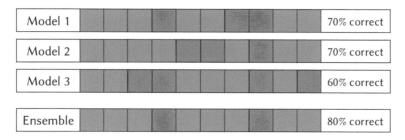

Figure 5. Example of three individual models attempting to predict ten outputs of either blue or red. The correct predictions were blue for all ten outputs. An ensemble formed by majority voting based on the three individual models yielded the highest prediction accuracy of 80%.

A systematic way to generate uncorrelated decision trees is a technique known as bootstrap aggregating.

10.4 Bootstrap Aggregating (Bagging)

We mentioned in the last chapter that, in constructing a decision tree, a dataset is repeatedly divided into subtrees, as guided by the best combination of variables. However, finding the right combination of variables can be difficult as decision trees are prone to the phenomenon of overfitting (explained in Chapter 1.3).

To overcome this, we could construct multiple decision trees by using random combinations and orders of variables, before aggregating the results from these trees to form a random forest.

Bootstrap aggregating (also termed as *bagging*) is used to create thousands of decision trees that are adequately different from each other. To ensure minimal correlation between trees, each tree is generated from a random subset of the training data, using a random subset of predictor variables. This allows us to grow trees that are dissimilar, but which still retain certain predictive powers. Figure 6 shows how the predictor variables, allowed for selection at each split on a tree, are restricted.

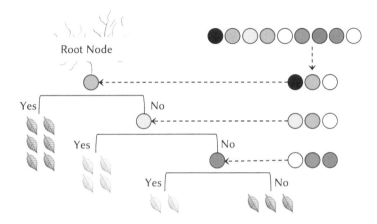

Figure 6. Creating a decision tree via bootstrap aggregating.

In Figure 6, there are a total of nine predictor variables, as represented by the different colors. A subset of predictor variables is randomly sampled from the original nine at each split, from which the decision tree algorithm then selects the best variable for the split.

By restricting the possible predictors for use at each split in the tree, we are able to generate dissimilar trees that prevent overfitting. To reduce overfitting even further, we could increase the number of trees in the random forest, which would result in a model that is more generalizable and accurate.

10.5 Limitations

No model is perfect. Choosing whether to use a random forest model is a trade-off between predictive power and interpretability of results.

Not interpretable. Random forests are considered *black boxes*, since they comprise randomly generated decision trees and are not led by clear prediction rules. For example, we could not know exactly how a random forest model reached its result—say, a prediction of a crime occurring at a specific place and time—except that a majority of its constituent decision trees came to the same conclusion. The lack of clarity on how its predictions are made could bring about ethical concerns when applied to areas such as medical diagnosis.

Nonetheless, random forests are widely used because they are easy to implement. They are particularly effective in situations where the accuracy of results is more crucial than their interpretability.

10.6 Summary

- A random forest often yields better prediction accuracy than decision trees because it leverages two techniques: *bootstrap aggregating* and *ensembling*.
- Bootstrap aggregating involves generating a series of un-correlated decision trees by randomly restricting variables during the splitting process, while ensembling involves combining the predictions of these trees.
- While results of a random forest are not interpretable, predictors can still be ranked according to their contributions to prediction accuracy.

11. Neural Networks

11.1 Building a Brain

Take a look at Figure 1 and guess what it shows.

Figure 1. Guess what this is.

You should be able to recognize it as a giraffe, even in its oddly fat form. Humans are empowered with brains that network some 80 billion neurons, allowing us to recognize objects easily even if presented differently from what we had seen before. These neurons work together to convert input signals (e.g. a giraffe picture) into corresponding output labels (e.g. a 'giraffe' label), and they are the inspiration behind the technique known as neural networks.

Neural networks form the basis of automated image recognition, and derivations of the technique have been shown to outperform humans in speed and accuracy. The recent popularity of neural networks can be attributed to three key reasons:

- **Advances in Data Storage and Sharing**. This has provided a larger amount of data that can be used to train neural networks, hence improving their performance.
- **Increased Computing Power**. Graphics processing units (GPUs), which run up to 150 times faster than central processing units (CPUs), were used mainly to display high quality computer images in games, but then discovered to be sturdy engines for training neural networks on large datasets.
- **Enhanced Algorithms**. While it remains difficult for machines to match the performance of the human brain, several techniques have been developed that improve their performance significantly. Several of these will be discussed in this chapter.

Automated image recognition is a fantastic example of the capabilities of neural networks. It is applied to many domains, including visual surveillance and autonomous vehicle navigation. It manifests even in smartphone applications that can recognize handwriting. Let us look at how we can train a neural network to do this.

11.2 Example: Recognizing Handwritten Digits

We used images of handwritten numerical digits from a database provided by the *Mixed National Institute of Standards and Technology* (MNIST). Example digits are shown in Figure 2.

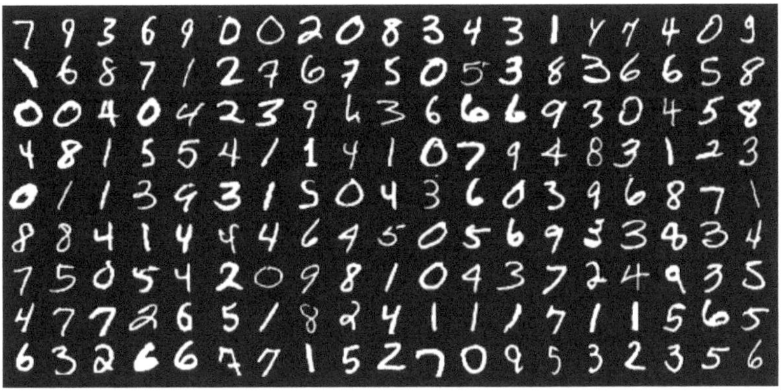

Figure 2. Handwritten digits in the MNIST database.

For a machine to read the images, we had to first translate them into pixels. Black pixels were given the value '0' and white pixels the value of '1', as shown in Figure 3. If the image was colored, we could have used values of its red, green and blue (RGB) hues instead.

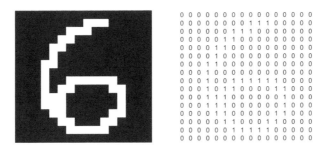

Figure 3. Translating an image into pixels.

Once the images have been quantified, the values could then be passed through a neural network. We fed the network a total of 10,000 handwritten digits, along with labels of the digits they actually represented. After the neural network had learned to associate images with their corresponding labels, we tested it to see if it could recognize 1000 new and unlabeled handwritten digits.

Of the 1000 handwritten digits, the neural network labelled 922 correctly—a 92.2% accuracy rate. Figure 4 shows a contingency table that we could use to examine identification errors.

		\multicolumn{10}{c}{Predicted Digit}		
		0	1	2	3	4	5	6	7	8	9	Total	%
Actual Digit	0	84	0	0	0	0	0	1	0	0	0	85	99
	1	0	125	0	0	0	0	1	0	0	0	126	99
	2	1	0	105	0	0	0	0	4	5	1	116	91
	3	0	0	3	96	0	6	0	1	0	1	107	90
	4	0	0	2	0	99	0	2	0	2	5	110	90
	5	2	0	0	5	0	77	1	0	1	1	87	89
	6	3	0	1	0	1	2	80	0	0	0	87	92
	7	0	3	3	0	1	0	0	90	0	2	99	91
	8	1	0	1	3	1	0	0	2	81	0	89	91
	9	0	0	0	0	1	0	0	6	2	85	94	90
	Total	91	128	115	104	103	85	85	103	91	95	1000	92

Figure 4. Contingency table summarizing the performance of the neural network. The first row tells us that 84 out of 85 images of digit '0' were correctly identified, and that the last one was wrongly identified as '6'. The last column indicates the accuracy rates.

From Figure 4, we can see that handwritten images of '0's and '1's were almost always identified correctly, while images of the digit '5' were the trickiest to identify. Let's take a closer look at the misidentified digits.

The digit '2' was misidentified as '7' or '8' about 8% of the time. While the human eye might easily recognize the digits shown in Figure 5, a neural network could be stumped by certain features such as the tail of the digit '2'. Interestingly, we can also observe that the neural network confused the digits '3' and '5' about 10% of the time (see Figure 6).

Despite these mistakes, the neural network performed much faster than a human, while still achieving a high overall accuracy rate.

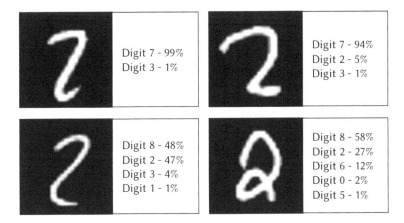

Figure 5. Misclassification of the digit '2'.

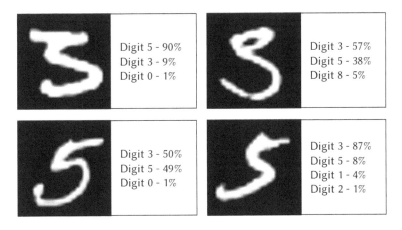

Figure 6. Misclassification of the digits '3' and '5'.

11.3 Components of a Neural Network

In order to recognize handwritten digits, a neural network uses multiple layers of neurons to process the input images for making predictions.

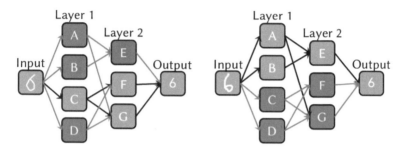

Figure 7. An example neural network fed with two different inputs but producing the same output. Activated neurons are in red.

Figure 7 shows how a neural network fed with images of the digit '6' in different handwriting used different neuron activation paths to generate the same prediction. Although each combination of activated neurons leads to only one prediction, each prediction could be reached by multiple combinations of activated neurons.

A typical neural network comprises the following components:

- **Input Layer.** This layer processes every pixel in an incoming image. As such, it is likely to have the same number of neurons as there are pixels in the image. For simplicity, we condensed these numerous neurons into a single node in Figure 7.

  To improve predictions, a **convolution layer** could be used. Instead of processing individual pixels, this layer identifies features made from combinations of pixels, such as the presence of a circle or an upward-pointing tail in the digit '6'. Since this style of analysis depends only on the presence of the features and not their locations, the neural network would still be able to recognize digits even if the key features are off-center—this property is known as *translational invariance*.

- **Hidden Layers**. After pixels enter the neural network, they undergo layers of transformations that attempt to increase their overall resemblance to images the network has seen before, for which labels are known. While accounting for more possible transformations might result in marginally higher accuracy, it comes at a cost of significantly longer processing time. Typically, a few layers would suffice. In each layer, the number of neurons should be proportional to the number of pixels in the image. In our example in the previous section, one hidden layer with 500 neurons was used.

- **Output Layer**. The final prediction is represented in this layer, which could consist of just one neuron, or as many as there are possible outcomes.

- **Loss Layer**. Although not shown in Figure 7, a *loss layer* would be present when a neural network is being trained. This layer, usually placed last, gives feedback on whether inputs have been identified correctly, and if not, the extent of error.

The loss layer is vital in training a neural network. If a correct prediction is made, feedback from the loss layer would reinforce the activated pathway that led to that prediction. If a wrong prediction is made, the error would be fed back across the pathway in a backward pass so that neurons along that path would re-calibrate their activation criteria in order to reduce the error. This process is called *backpropagation*.

Through this iterative training process, the neural network learns to associate input signals with the correct output labels, and these learned associations would be programmed as *activation rules* within each neuron. Hence, to increase the accuracy of a neural network, we need to tune the components governing its activation rules.

11.4 Activation Rules

To generate predictions, neurons along a neural pathway need to be activated in turn. The activation of each neuron is governed by its *activation rule*, which specifies the source and strength of input signals that a neuron has to receive before it is activated. This rule would be fine-tuned during the training of the neural network.

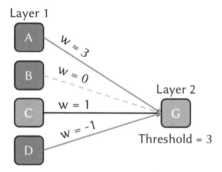

Figure 8. Example of a neuron's activation rule.

Figure 8 illustrates a mock activation rule for neuron G from the first scenario in Figure 7. After training, the neural network has learned that neuron G is associated with neurons A, C, and D from the preceding layer. As such, any activations in these three neurons would be transmitted as input signals to neuron G.

Associations possess varying strengths, which are also known as *weights*, denoted as *w*. For instance, we can see in Figure 8 that activating neuron A would send a stronger signal ($w = 3$) to neuron G than activating neuron C ($w = 1$). Associations are also directional, such that activating neuron D ($w = -1$) would actually decrease the input signals transmitted to neuron G.

To determine the total input signal fed to neuron G, we sum all the weights from activated neurons in the preceding layer that it associates with. If the resulting signal received crosses a determined threshold, neuron G would be activated. In Figure 8, the resulting signal strength is 2, i.e. 3 + (-1). Since neuron G has a threshold of 3, it remains inactivated in this case.

Learning the right values for weights and thresholds is essential for good activation rules that lead to accurate predictions. In addition, a neural network's other parameters also require tuning, such as the number of hidden layers and number of neurons within each layer. To optimize these parameters, gradient descent (see Chapter 6.3) could be used.

11.5 Limitations

Despite its potential ability to emulate the human brain, neural networks still suffer from several drawbacks. To overcome them, a variety of techniques have been developed.

Large Sample Size Requirement. The complexity of a neural network enables it to recognize inputs with intricate features, but it can only do so when there are large amounts of data available to train on. If the training set is too small, overfitting (see Chapter 1.3) might occur. But if obtaining more training data is difficult, we could use the following techniques to minimize the risk of overfitting:

- **Subsampling**. To reduce the sensitivity of neurons to noise, inputs to the network could be 'smoothened' through a process known as *subsampling*. This is achieved by taking averages over a sample of the signal. If we are performing this on images for instance, we could reduce image size, or lower color contrast across RGB channels.
- **Distortions**. If there is a lack of training data, we could create more data by introducing distortions to each image. By treating each distorted image as a new input, we would expand the size of our training data. Distortions used should reflect those present in the original dataset. In handwritten

digits, for instance, images could be rotated to emulate how some people write at an angle, or stretched and squeezed at certain points (known as *elastic deformation*) to simulate uncontrolled oscillations of the hand muscles.

- **Dropout**. If there are few training examples to learn from, neurons might have fewer opportunities to form associations with different neurons, leading to overfitting as small neuron clusters develop an over-reliance on each other. To counter this, we could randomly exclude half of the neurons during a training cycle. These dropped neurons would be deactivated, with the remaining neurons behaving as if the dropped neurons did not exist. A different set of dropped neurons would then be used in the next training iteration. This is how the *dropout* technique forces different combinations of neurons to work together, so as to uncover more features from the training examples.

Computationally Expensive. Training a neural network that comprises thousands of neurons could take a long time. While an easy solution would be to upgrade our computing hardware, this would be costly. An alternative solution would be to tweak our algorithms to trade significantly faster processing speed for slightly lower prediction accuracy. Here are some ways to do this:

- **Stochastic gradient descent**. In the classic gradient descent algorithm (see Chapter 6.3), we cycle through *all* training examples to update a single parameter in an iteration. As this is time-consuming with large datasets, an alternative would be to use just *one* training example in each iteration to update the parameter. This technique is known as *stochastic gradient descent*, and while the resulting parameter values might not be exactly optimal, they usually yield decent accuracy.
- **Mini-batch gradient descent**. While referencing just one training example in each iteration could be faster, the trade-off is that the resulting parameter estimate could be less

precise and the algorithm might be less likely to converge, resulting in a parameter that oscillates about the optimal value. A middle-ground solution would be to reference a subset of training examples for each iteration, and this technique is known as *mini-batch gradient descent*.

- **Fully connected layers**. As we add more neurons, the number of possible neural pathways increases exponentially. To avoid examining all the possible combinations, we could leave neurons in the initial layers—which process smaller, low-level features—as partially connected. Only in the final layers—where larger, high-level features are processed—do we fully connect neurons in adjacent layers.

Not Interpretable. Neural networks consist of multiple layers, each with hundreds of neurons governed by different activation rules. This makes it difficult to pinpoint a specific combination of input signals that would result in a correct prediction. This is unlike techniques such as regression (see Chapter 6), for which significant predictors could be clearly identified and compared. A neural network's *black box* characteristic could make it difficult to justify its use, especially in ethical decisions. Nonetheless, work is ongoing to dissect the training progress at each neural layer to examine how individual input signals influence resulting predictions.

Despite its limitations, the effectiveness of neural networks continues to spur their deployment in cutting-edge technology such as virtual assistants and autonomous driving. Beyond emulating humans, neural networks have already superseded our abilities in some areas, as seen in the 2015 landmark match in the board game *Go*, during which a human player lost to Google's neural network. As we continue to refine algorithms and push the boundaries of computing power, neural networks will play an integral role in the age of *Internet-of-Things*, by connecting and automating our daily tasks.

11.6 Summary

- A neural network comprises layers of neurons. During training, neurons in the first layer are activated by input data, and these activations are propagated to neurons in subsequent layers, eventually reaching the final output layer to make predictions.
- Whether a neuron is activated depends on the strength and source of activation it receives, as set out in its *activation rule*. Activation rules are refined using feedback on prediction accuracy, through a process called *backpropagation.*
- Neural networks perform best when large datasets and advanced computing hardware are available. Results would nonetheless be largely uninterpretable.

12. A/B Testing and Multi-Armed Bandits

12.1 Basics of A/B testing

Imagine that you ran an online store, and you wanted to put up advertisements to notify people of an ongoing sale. Which statement would you use?

- Up to 50% discount on items!
- Half-price on selected items

Although both statements mean the same thing, one could be more persuasive than the other. For instance, is it better to use an exclamation mark to convey excitement, and is the numerical figure of '50%' more compelling than the term 'half-price'?

To find out what works, you could display each version of your ad to 100 people in a pilot trial, to see how many eventually clicked on each ad. The ad that garnered more clicks would appear to attract more buyers, and thus should be used for the rest of your advertising campaign. This procedure is known as *A/B testing*, in which the effectiveness of ad versions *A* and *B* are compared.

12.2 Limitations of A/B testing

There are two problems with the A/B testing method:

Results could be a fluke. By sheer chance, a lousier ad could outperform a better ad. To be more certain of the results, we could increase the number of people we show each ad version to—but this leads to a second problem.

Potential loss of revenue. By increasing the number of people to whom we show each ad version from 100 to 200, we would also end up displaying the lousier ad to twice as many people, potentially losing buyers who might have been persuaded by the better ad.

These two problems represent the trade-off in A/B testing: *exploration* versus *exploitation*. If you increase the number of people to test your ads on (exploration), you could eventually become more certain about which ad is better, but you would lose potential customers who might have made purchases had they seen the better ad (exploitation).

How do we balance this trade-off?

12.3 Epsilon–Decreasing Strategy

While A/B testing involves exploring which is the better ad before committing the rest of the campaign to exploiting that ad, we need not actually wait to finish exploration before commencing exploitation.

If Ad A had garnered more clicks than Ad B among the first 100 viewers, we could increase the exposure of Ad A to 60% of the next 100 viewers, while decreasing that of Ad B to 40%. This would allow us to start exploiting the initial result showing Ad A's better performance, without preventing us from continuing to explore the small possibility of improvement in Ad B's performance. As more evidence tilts the result in Ad A's favor, we could progressively show more of Ad A and less of Ad B.

This approach leverages the *epsilon-decreasing strategy*. *Epsilon* refers to the proportion of time spent exploring an alternative, to ensure that it is indeed less effective. Since we decrease epsilon as our confidence in the better ad is reinforced, this technique belongs to a class of algorithms known as *reinforcement learning*.

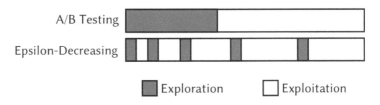

Figure 1. An A/B test comprises one exploration phase followed by one exploitation phase, whereas an epsilon-decreasing strategy intersperses exploration with exploitation, with more exploration at the start and less toward the end.

12.4 Example: Multi-Arm Bandits

A typical example used to illustrate the difference between A/B testing and the epsilon-decreasing strategy is slot machine play. Given that slot machines have different payout rates, a gambler's aim would then be to choose which machine to play in order to increase his overall payout.

Figure 2. A one-arm bandit.

Slot machines have been nicknamed *one-arm bandits* since they appear to cheat players of money with each arm pull. As such, choosing which slot machine to play is known as a *multi-arm bandit* problem, which is a term that now refers to any problem on resource allocation, such as deciding which ad to show, which topics to revise before an exam, or which drug study to fund.

Imagine that there are two slot machines to choose from, A and B. We have enough money to play a total of 2000 rounds across both machines. In each round, we pull the arm of one machine, which would either win us $1 or return us nothing.

Machine	Payout Rate
A	0.5
B	0.4

Table 1. Machine payout rates.

The chance of payout is 50% for Machine A, and 40% for Machine B. However, we do not know these probabilities. The question, then, is how we should play to maximize our winnings.

Let's compare possible strategies:

Total Exploration. If we played each machine at random, we would obtain $900 on average.

A/B Testing. If we used A/B testing to explore which slot machine has a higher payout for the first 200 rounds, and then exploit the better machine for the next 1800 rounds, we would potentially get $976 on average. But there is a catch: since the payout rates for both machines are similar, there is actually an 8% chance we might misidentify Machine B as the one with the higher payout.

To reduce the risk of an identification error, we could extend exploration over 500 rounds. This may lower the misidentification risk to 1%, but our resulting winnings would also drop to an average of $963.

Epsilon-Decreasing Strategy. If we used an epsilon-decreasing strategy to begin exploiting a seemingly better machine as we continue exploring, we could win $984 on average while tolerating a 4% chance of misidentification. We could probably decrease the risk of misidentification by increasing the rate of exploration (i.e. value of epsilon), but as before, this would decrease our average winnings.

Total Exploitation. If we had insider knowledge that Machine A had a higher payout, we could exploit it from the very start and get $1000 on average. But this is not (easily) realizable.

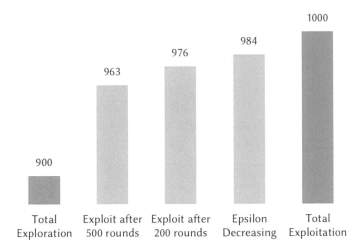

Figure 3. Comparing payouts from different playing strategies.

From Figure 3, it is clear that in the absence of insider knowledge, the epsilon-decreasing strategy yields the highest winnings. Moreover, for a large number of games, a mathematical property called convergence ensures that this strategy would surely reveal the better machine.

12.5 Fun Fact: Sticking to the Winner

An interesting application of the multi-arm bandit problem is in sports. During his tenure with the famed soccer club *Manchester United*, manager Louis van Gaal adopted an unconventional strategy to decide how his players would take penalty shoots.

The first player appointed to take penalties would continue to do so, until he missed. Following this, the next player would take over until he missed, and so on. This strategy is known as *sticking to the winner*.

If we saw our slot machines in Table 1 as akin to soccer players with unknown goal-scoring rates, sticking to a machine when we win and switching when we lose would give us an average winning of about $909, which is only slightly better than playing randomly. If one switched machines frequently, there would be too much exploration and too little exploitation. Furthermore, sticking to the winner would overlook a machine's history of performance by evaluating it solely by its last game. This strategy is obviously less than ideal.

12.6 Limitations of an Epsilon–Decreasing Strategy

While an epsilon-decreasing strategy appears superior, it is also subject to limitations that render it more difficult to implement as compared to A/B testing.

To use an epsilon-decreasing strategy, it is crucial to control the value of epsilon. If epsilon decreases too slowly, we could miss out on exploiting the better machine. If done too quickly, we might identify the wrong machine to exploit.

The optimal rate of decrease for epsilon depends heavily on how different the payout rates of the two machines are. If highly similar, as in Table 1, epsilon should be decreased slowly. To compute epsilon, a method called *Thompson sampling* could be used.

An epsilon-decreasing strategy also depends on the following assumptions:

1. **Payout rate is constant over time**. An ad might be popular in the morning but not at night, while another might be moderately popular throughout the day. If we compared both ads in the morning, we would have falsely concluded the first ad to be better.
2. **Payout rate is independent of previous plays**. If an ad is presented multiple times, a customer might grow curious and hence be more likely to click on it. This means that repeated exploration might be required to reveal true payouts.
3. **Minimal delay between playing a machine and observing the payout**. If an ad is sent via email, potential buyers might take a few days to respond. This would prevent us from knowing the true results of our exploration immediately, and any exploitation attempts in the meantime would be based on incomplete information.

Nonetheless, if either the 2nd or 3rd assumption was violated by both ads being compared, the effect of any errors could be cancelled out. For instance, if two ads were sent via email, response delays would be present for both ads, and the comparison would remain fair.

12.7 Summary

- The multi-armed bandit problem deals with the question of how to best allocate resources—whether to exploit known returns, or to search for better alternatives.
- One solution is to first explore available options, before allocating all remaining resources to the best-performing option. This strategy is called *A/B testing*.
- Another solution is to steadily increase resources allocated to the best-performing option over time. This is known as the *epsilon-decreasing strategy*.
- While the epsilon-decreasing strategy gives higher returns than A/B testing in most cases, it is not easy to determine the optimal rate to update the allocation of resources.

Appendix

A. Overview of Unsupervised Learning Algorithms

		k-Means Clustering	Principal Component Analysis	Association Rules	Louvain Method	PageRank
Input	Binary Values			✓		
	Continuous Values	✓	✓			
	Nodes & Edges				✓	✓
Output	Categories	✓	✓		✓	
	Associations			✓		
	Ranks					✓

B. Overview of Supervised Learning Algorithms

		Regression Analysis	k-Nearest Neighbors	Support Vector Machine	Decision Tree	Random Forests	Neural Networks
Prediction	Binary Outcomes	✓	✓	✓	✓	✓	✓
	Categorical Outcomes		✓		✓	✓	✓
	Class Probabilities	✓	✓		✓	✓	✓
	Continuous Outcomes	✓	✓		✓	✓	✓
	Non-linear Relationships		✓	✓	✓	✓	✓
Analysis	Large Number of Variables			✓	✓	✓	✓
	Simple to Use	✓	✓		✓	✓	
	Fast Computation	✓			✓		
Results	Highly Accurate					✓	✓
	Interpretable	✓	✓		✓		

C. List of Tuning Parameters

	Tuning Parameters
Regression Analysis	• Regularization parameter (for lasso and ridge regression)
k-Nearest Neighbors	• Number of nearest neighbors
Support Vector Machine	• Soft margin constant • Kernel parameters • Insensitivity parameter
Decision Tree	• Minimum size of terminal nodes • Maximum number of terminal nodes • Maximum tree depth
Random Forests	• All parameters of a decision tree • Number of trees • Number of variables to select at each split
Neural Networks	• Number of hidden layers • Number of neurons in each layer • Number of training iterations • Learning rate • Initial weights

D. More Evaluation Metrics

Evaluation metrics vary in how they define and penalize different types of prediction errors. This section introduces several more common metrics, in addition to those covered in Chapter 1.4.

Classification Metrics

Area Under the Receiver Operating Characteristic (AUROC) Curve. Also known more generically as *Area Under the Curve* (AUC), this metric allows us to choose between maximizing the *true positive rate* or minimizing the *false positive rate.*

- **True Positive Rate (TPR)** refers to the proportion of all positive points that were correctly classified as positive:

  TPR = TP / (TP + FN)

- **False Positive Rate (FPR)** refers to the proportion of all negative points that were incorrectly classified as positive:

  FPR = FP / (FP + TN)

In an extreme case, we could choose to fully maximize the true positive rate, where TPR is set to 1, by predicting all points to be positive. While this would eliminate false negatives, it would significantly increase the number of false positives. In other words, there is a trade-off between minimizing false positives and maximizing true positives.

This trade-off could be visualized using a *Receiver Operating Characteristic* (ROC) curve, as shown in Figure 1.

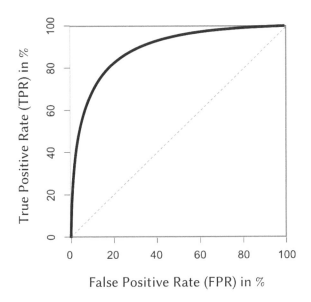

Figure 1. An ROC curve showing the trade-off between maximizing true positives and minimizing false positives.

The performance of the model is measured using the area under the ROC curve, thus giving the metric its name. The more accurate the model, the closer the curve would be to the plot's top-left edges. A perfect prediction model would generate a curve with an AUC of 1, equivalent to the entire plot area. In contrast, the performance of a model with random predictions would be represented by the diagonal dotted line, with an AUC of 0.5.

In practice, we could identify the best prediction model as the one yielding the highest AUC, and its ROC curve could then be used to select an appropriate threshold for the TPR or FPR that we would be willing to tolerate.

Now, while the ROC curve allows us to be selective about the type of error we wish to avoid, we could also penalize all wrong predictions in general using a logarithmic loss metric.

Logarithmic Loss (Log Loss). Predictions for binary and categorical variables are generally expressed as a probability, such as the probability that a customer would buy fish. The closer this probability is to 100%, the more *confident* the model is that the customer would purchase fish. The log loss metric takes advantage of this measure of confidence to calibrate its penalties for wrong predictions—specifically, the more confident a model is of a wrong prediction, the heavier its penalty on the log loss metric.

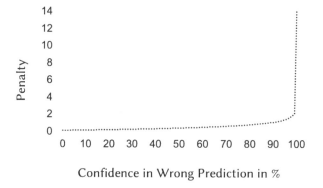

Confidence in Wrong Prediction in %

Figure 2. Log loss penalty increases as a model's confidence in a wrong prediction increases.

Figure 2 shows the drastic increase in penalty as confidence in a wrong prediction approaches the upper limit. For example, if our model predicts an 80% chance that a customer would buy fish, but this turns out to be wrong, we would be penalized 0.7 points. If our model had instead predicted a 99% chance that fish would be bought, our penalty would more than double to 2 points.

Due to its ability to adjust penalties based on prediction confidence, the log loss metric is commonly used in cases where wrong predictions are particularly detrimental.

Regression Metrics

Mean Absolute Error (MAE). A simple way to evaluate a regression model is to penalize all errors equally, by taking the average gap between predicted and actual values across all data points. This metric is called the *mean absolute error.*

Root Mean Squared Logarithmic Error (RMSLE). In Chapter 1.4, we introduced the root mean squared error metric, which amplifies the penalty for large errors. In addition to the magnitude of error, we could also account for the direction of error using the *root mean squared logarithmic error* (RMSLE) metric. The RMSLE could be used if we wish to avoid under-estimates more than over-estimates, such as when predicting demand for umbrellas on a rainy day. Under-estimation would result in unhappy customers and lost revenue, whereas over-estimation would lead only to extra inventory.

Glossary

A/B Testing. A strategy to compare the returns from two products, A and B. The process starts with an exploration phase, where both products are tested at the same rate. After which, the better product is identified and all resources are devoted to it to maximize returns in an exploitation phase. The degree of trade-off between exploration (to check for better alternatives) and exploitation (to increase potential rewards) is a central decision for the conduct of any A/B test.

Activation Rule. A criterion that specifies the source and strength of input signals that a neuron has to receive before it is activated. Neuron activations are propagated through a neural network to generate predictions.

Apriori Principle. A rule which states that if an itemset is infrequent, then any larger itemset containing it must also be infrequent. It is a technique used to reduce the number of configurations we need to examine in measuring frequency and associations of items.

Association Rules. An unsupervised learning technique that discovers how data points are associated with each other, such as identifying items that are frequently bought together. There are three common measures of association:

- *Support* of {X} indicates how frequently item X appears
- *Confidence* of {X->Y} indicates how frequently item Y appears when item X is present
- *Lift* of {X->Y} indicates how frequently items X and Y appear together, while accounting for how frequently each would appear on its own

Backpropagation. A process of sending feedback in a neural network on whether a prediction was accurate. If a prediction was wrong, the error would be sent across the neural pathway in a backward pass so that neurons along that path would re-calibrate their activation criteria in order to reduce the error.

Best-Fit Line. A trend line that passes through or sits close to as many data points as possible.

Black Box. A term used to describe a prediction model that is uninterpretable, in that it does not have a clear formula for deriving its predictions.

Bootstrap Aggregating (Bagging). A technique to create thousands of uncorrelated decision trees, from which predictions are averaged to prevent overfitting. Each tree is generated from a random subset of the training data, using a random subset of predictor variables for selection at each tree branch.

Classification. A class of supervised learning techniques where we predict binary or categorical values.

Confusion Matrix. A metric to evaluate the accuracy of classification predictions. Apart from overall classification accuracy, the matrix shows rates of false positives and false negatives.

Correlation. A metric to measure the linear association between two variables. Correlation coefficients range from -1 to 1, and provide two pieces of information: 1) strength of association, which is maximized at -1 or 1 and minimized at 0, as well as 2) direction of association, which is positive when the two variables move together in the same direction, and negative otherwise.

Cross-Validation. A technique to maximize the availability of data for validation by dividing the dataset into several segments that are used to test the model repeatedly. In a single iteration, all but one of the segments are used to train a prediction model, which is then tested on the last segment. This process is repeated until each segment has been used as the test segment exactly once. The final estimate of the model's prediction accuracy is taken as the average of that across all iterations.

Decision Tree. A supervised learning technique that makes predictions by asking a sequence of binary questions to repeatedly partition data points to obtain homogeneous groups. While easy to understand and visualize, decision trees are prone to overfitting.

Dimension Reduction. A process of decreasing the number of variables in the data, such as by combining highly correlated ones.

Dropout. A technique to prevent overfitting a neural network model, where we randomly exclude a different subset of neurons during each training cycle, forcing different combinations of neurons to work together to uncover more features.

Ensembling. A technique to combine multiple prediction models to improve accuracy. It works well because models that yield accurate predictions tend to reinforce each other, while wrong predictions cancel each other out.

Epsilon-Decreasing Strategy. A reinforcement learning technique for allocating resources that intersperses two phases: 1) exploring for better alternatives, and 2) exploiting known returns. Epsilon is the proportion of time spent exploring alternatives, and is decreased as more information is gained on which is the best alternative.

Feature Engineering. A process of generating new variables creatively, such as by recoding a single variable, or by combining multiple ones.

Gradient Boosting. A supervised learning technique that generates multiple decision trees by selecting different combinations of binary questions to grow each tree branch. Binary questions are selected strategically (instead of randomly, as in random forests), such that prediction accuracy for each subsequent tree improves. Predictions from individual trees are then combined, with latter trees given a heavier weight, to generate final predictions.

Gradient Descent. A technique to tune model parameters. It makes an initial estimate on a set of parameter values, before starting an iterative process of applying these estimates to every data point to get predictions, and then revising the estimates to reduce overall prediction error.

k-Means Clustering. An unsupervised learning technique that groups similar data points together, where k is the number of groups to be identified.

k-Nearest Neighbors. A supervised learning technique that classifies a data point by referring to classifications of other data points it is closest to, where k is the number of data points to reference.

Kernel Trick. A technique to project data points onto a higher dimension, where data points can be separated by a straight boundary. These straight boundaries are simpler to compute, and are also easily translated into curved ones when projected back down onto a lower dimension.

Louvain Method. An unsupervised learning technique that identifies clusters in a network, in a way that maximizes interactions within clusters and minimizes those between clusters.

Multi-Arm Bandit Problem. A term used to refer to any problem on resource allocation, such as deciding which slot machine to place bets on. The term was inspired by the moniker for slot machines— one-arm bandits—as they appear to cheat players of money with each arm pull.

Multicollinearity. A problem in regression analysis where inclusion of highly correlated predictors result in distorted interpretations of regression weights.

Neural Network. A supervised learning technique that uses layers of neurons to transmit activations for learning and making predictions. While highly accurate, results are largely uninterpretable due to its complexity.

Overfitting. A phenomenon where a prediction model is overly sensitive and mistakes random variations in data as persistent patterns. An overfitted model would yield highly accurate predictions for current data, but would be less generalizable to future data.

PageRank. An algorithm that identifies dominant nodes in a network. It ranks nodes based on their number of links, as well as the strength and source of those links.

Parameter Tuning. A process of adjusting an algorithm's settings to improve the accuracy of the resulting model, much like tuning a radio for the right frequency channel.

Principal Component Analysis. An unsupervised learning technique that reduces the number of variables we have to analyze by combining the most informative variables in our data into new variables called principal components.

Random Forest. A supervised learning technique that generates multiple decision trees by selecting different combinations of binary questions at random to grow each tree branch. Predictions from individual trees are then aggregated to generate final predictions.

Recursive Partitioning. A process of repeatedly splitting a data sample to obtain homogeneous groups, as used in decision trees.

Regression Analysis. A supervised learning technique that finds the best-fit trend line that passes through or sits close to as many data points as possible. The trend line is derived from a weighted combination of predictors.

Regularization. A technique to prevent overfitting a prediction model by introducing a penalty parameter that artificially inflates prediction error with any increase in the model's complexity. This enables us to account for both complexity and accuracy in optimizing model parameters.

Reinforcement Learning. A class of machine learning algorithms that is used when we want to make predictions based on patterns in our data, and to continuously improve those predictions as more results come in.

Root Mean Squared Error. A metric to evaluate the accuracy of regression predictions. It is particularly useful in cases where we want to avoid large errors. As each individual error is squared, large errors are amplified, rendering the metric extremely sensitive to outliers.

Scree Plot. A graph used to determine how many groups we wish to keep. Groups can range from data clusters to reduced dimensions. The optimal number of groups is usually determined by the location of a kink, which is a sharp bend in the scree plot. Beyond this point, allowing more groups might yield less generalizable results.

Standardization. A process that shifts variables onto a uniform standard scale, analogous to expressing each variable in terms of its percentiles.

Subsampling. A technique to prevent overfitting a neural network model, where we 'smoothen' out the input training data by taking averages. If we are performing this on images for instance, we could reduce image size or lower color contrast.

Supervised Learning. A class of machine learning algorithms that is used to make predictions. These algorithms are supervised because we want them to base their predictions on pre-existing patterns in our data.

Support Vector Machine. A supervised learning technique that classifies data points into two groups by drawing a boundary down the middle between the peripheral data points, also called support vectors, of both groups. It employs the kernel trick to efficiently derive curved boundaries.

Test Dataset. A data sample that is used to assess the accuracy and generalizability of a prediction model. The test dataset is withheld initially while the model is generated from a training dataset.

Training Dataset. A data sample that is used to discover potentially predictive relationships to generate a prediction model. The model is then assessed using a separate test dataset.

Translational Invariance. A property of convolutional neural networks, where image features are recognized regardless of where they are positioned on the image.

Underfitting. A phenomenon where a prediction model is too insensitive, and overlooks underlying patterns. An underfitted model is likely to neglect significant trends, which would cause it to give less accurate predictions for both current and future data.

Unsupervised Learning. A class of machine learning algorithms that is used to find hidden patterns in our data. These algorithms are unsupervised because we do not know what patterns to look out for and thus leave them to be uncovered by the algorithms.

Validation. An assessment of how accurate our model is in predicting new data. It involves splitting the current dataset into two parts: the first part serves as a training dataset to generate and tune our prediction model, while the second part acts as a proxy for new data and is used as a test dataset to assess our model's accuracy.

Variable. Information that describes your data points. Variables are also known as attributes, features, or dimensions. There are different types of variables:

- **Binary**. The simplest type of variable, with only two possible options (e.g. male vs. female).
- **Categorical**. A variable that is used to represent more than two options (e.g. ethnicity).
- **Integer**. A variable that is used to represent whole numbers (e.g. age).
- **Continuous**. The most detailed type of variable, representing numbers with decimal places (e.g. price).

Data Sources and References

Personality of Facebook Users (*k*-Means Clustering)

Stillwell, D., & Kosinski, M. (2012). *myPersonality Project* [Data files and description]. Sample dataset can be retrieved from http://data miningtutorial.com

Kosinski, M., Matz, S., Gosling, S., Popov, V., & Stillwell, D. (2015). *Facebook as a Social Science Research Tool: Opportunities, Challenges, Ethical Considerations and Practical Guidelines.* American Psychologist.

Food Nutrients (Principal Component Analysis)

Agricultural Research Service, United States Department of Agriculture (2015). *USDA Food Composition Databases* [Data]. Retrieved from https://ndb.nal.usda.gov/ndb/nutrients/index

Grocery Transactions (Association Rules)

Dataset is included in the following R package: Hahsler, M., Buchta, C., Gruen, B., & Hornik, K. (2016). *arules: Mining Association Rules and Frequent Itemsets.* R package version 1.5-0. https://CRAN.R-project.org/package=arules

Hahsler, M., Hornik, K., & Reutterer, T. (2006). *Implications of Probabilistic Data Modeling for Mining Association Rules.* In Spiliopoulou, M., Kruse, R., Borgelt, C., Nürnberger, A.,& Gaul, W. Eds., *From Data and Information Analysis to Knowledge Engineering, Studies in Classification, Data Analysis, and Knowledge Organization.* pp. 598-605. Berlin, Germany: Springer-Verlag.

Hahsler, M., & Chelluboina, S. (2011). Visualizing Association Rules: Introduction to the R-extension Package arulesViz. *R Project Module*, 223-238.

Weapon Trade (Network Graphs)

Stockholm International Peace Research Institute (2015). *Trade Registers* [Data]. Retrieved from http://armstrade.sipri.org/armstrade/page/trade_register.php

House Prices (Regression Analysis)

Harrison, D., & Rubinfeld, D. (1993). *Boston Housing Data* [Data file and description]. Retrieved from https://archive.ics.uci.edu/ml/datasets/Housing

Harrison, D., & Rubinfeld, D. (1978). Hedonic Prices and the Demand for Clean Air. *Journal of Environmental Economics and Management, 5*, 81-102.

Wine Composition (*k*-Nearest Neighbors)

Forina, M., et al. (1998). *Wine Recognition Data* [Data file and description]. Retrieved from http://archive.ics.uci.edu/ml/datasets/Wine

Cortez, P., Cerdeira, A., Almeida, F., Matos, T., & Reis, J. (2009). Modeling Wine Preferences by Data Mining from Physicochemical Properties. *Decision Support Systems, 47*(4), 547-553.

Heart Disease (Support Vector Machine)

Robert Detrano (M.D., Ph.D), from Virginia Medical Center, Long Beach and Cleveland Clinic Foundation (1988). *Heart Disease Database (Cleveland)* [Data file and description]. Retrieved from https://archive.ics.uci.edu/ml/datasets/Heart+Disease

Detrano, R., et al. (1989). International Application of a New Probability Algorithm for the Diagnosis of Coronary Artery Disease. *The American Journal of Cardiology, 64*(5), 304-310.

Titanic Survivors (Decision Tree)

British Board of Trade Inquiry (1990). *Titanic Data* [Data file and description]. Retrieved from http://www.public.iastate.edu/~hofma nn/data/titanic.html

Report on the Loss of the 'Titanic' (S.S.) (1990). British Board of Trade Inquiry Report (reprint), Gloucester, UK: Allan Sutton Publishing and are discussed in Dawson, R. J. M. (1995). The 'Unusual Episode' Data Revisited. *Journal of Statistics Education, 3*(3).

Crime in San Francisco (Random Forest)

SF OpenData, City and County of San Francisco (2016). *Crime Incidents* [Data]. Retrieved from https://data.sfgov.org/Public-Safety/Map-Crime-Incidents-from-1-Jan-2003/gxxq-x39z

Weather in San Francisco (Random Forest)

National Oceanic and Atmospheric Administration, National Centers for Environmental Information (2016). *Quality Controlled Local Climatological Data (QCLCD)* [Data file and description]. Retrieved from https://www.ncdc.noaa.gov/qclcd/QCLCD?prior=N

Handwritten Digits (Neural Networks)

LeCun, Y., & Cortes, C. (1998). *The MNIST Database of Handwritten Digits* [Data file and description]. Retrieved from http://yann.lecun .com/exdb/mnist

LeCun, Y., Bottou, L., Bengio, Y., & Haffner, P. (1998). Gradient-based Learning Applied to Document Recognition. *Proceedings of the IEEE, 86*(11), 2278-2324.

For more open datasets, visit:

Lichman, M. (2013). *UCI Machine Learning Repository.* Irvine, CA: University of California, School of Information and Computer Science. Retrieved from http://archive.ics.uci.edu/ml

About the Authors

Annalyn Ng graduated from the University of Michigan (Ann Arbor), where she also was an undergraduate statistics tutor. She then completed her MPhil degree with the University of Cambridge Psychometrics Centre, where she mined social media data for targeted advertising and programmed cognitive tests for job recruitment. Disney Research later roped her into their behavioral sciences team, where she examined psychological profiles of consumers.

Kenneth Soo is due to complete his MS degree in Statistics at Stanford University by mid-2017. He was the top student for all three years of his undergraduate class in Mathematics, Operational Research, Statistics and Economics (MORSE) at the University of Warwick, where he was also a research assistant with the Operational Research & Management Sciences Group, working on bi-objective robust optimization with applications in networks subject to random failures.